The Revenge of
Sherlock Hol

A musical mystery

Book, Music and Lyrics by
Leslie Bricusse

Samuel French — London
New York - Toronto - Hollywood

THE REVENGE OF
SHERLOCK HOLMES

This printed version was produced at the Bristol Old Vic on 11th March, 1993 with the following cast:

Sherlock Holmes	Robert Powell
Professor Moriarty	Peter Brollow
Dr Watson	Roy Barraclough
Inspector Lestrade	James Head
Mrs Hudson	Sarah Hay
Sir Jevons Jarndyce	Stephen Earle
The Irregulars:	
Wiggins	John Tobias
Mossop	Ray Strachan
Billy Higgins	Tim Flannigan
Potatoes Clark	Sean Kingsley
Lofty Daniels	Philip Hazelby
Mick O'Reilly	Andrew Tyler
Bert the Fishmonger	Paul Mead
Duchess of Monmouth	Paula Margetson
Bella Spellgrove	Louise English
Mrs Moriarty	Marilyn Cutts
Maria	Kathryn Hare
PC Bottomley	Andrew Tyler
PC Tomkins	Philip Hazelby
Dr "Boffy" Martingdale	David Oakley
Street Girl	Lorinda King
Newsgirl	Cheryl Jane King
Market Porter	David Langham

Directed by Bob Tomson
Designed by Mick Bearwish
Musical Director Stuart Pedlar

The original version was first presented at the Northcott Theatre, Exeter on 18th October, 1988. It was subsequently presented by D & J Arlon for Showplay Ltd in association with Stage and Screen Music at the Cambridge Theatre, London, on 24th April 1989, with the following cast:

Sherlock Holmes	Ron Moody
Dr Watson	Derek Waring
Bella Spellgrove	Liz Robertson
Mrs Moriarty	Eileen Battye
Inspector Lestrade	Roger Llewellyn
Mrs Hudson	Julia Sutton
Dr "Boffy" Martingdale	John Gower
Duchess of Monmouth	Sally Mates
Sir Jevons Jarndyce	Lewis Barber
Professor James Moriarty	Terry Williams
Fred Wiggins	James Francis-Johnston
Harry Mossop	Derek Cullen
Potatoes Clark	Jamie Hinde
Billy Higgins	Luke Hope
Lofty Daniel	Paul Loxton
Mick O'Reilly	Stephen Matthews
Maria	Erike Vincent

Ensemble: John Alexander, Margaret Bankier, Michael Conran, Bronwen Davies, Bonnie Hassell, Peter Johnston, Gaynor Martine, Sally Mates, Terry Mitchell, Jenny Sawyer, Debra Stables, Erike Vincent, Terry Williams, Michael Winsor, Kate-Alice Woodbridge

Directed by George Roman
Designed by Sean Cavanagh
Musical Director Cyril Ornadel

CHARACTERS

Professor Moriarty
Sherlock Holmes
Dr Watson
Bella Spellgrove
Mrs Hudson
Inspector Lestrade
Mrs Moriarty

The Baker Street Irregulars:
Fred Wiggins
Harry Mossop
Potatoes Clark

Dr "Boffy" Martingdale
Sir Jevons Jarndyce
Duchess of Monmouth
Maria
PC Bottomley
PC Tomkins

Policemen, Petty Thieves, Down-and-outs, Salvation Army, etc. to be played by the Company

MUSICAL NUMBERS

ACT I

1	**Sherlock Holmes**	Mrs Hudson, Watson, Irregulars
2	**Without Him, There Can Be No Me**	Watson, Holmes
3	**Anything You Want to Know**	Irregulars
3a	**Anything You Want to Know (Reprise)**	Irregulars
4	**Look Around You**	Holmes, Watson, Lestrade
5	**London Is London**	Irregulars
5a	**London Is London (Reprise)**	Irregulars
6	**Her Face**	Watson
7	**Men Like You**	Bella, Holmes
8	**A Lousy Life**	Mrs Hudson
9	**I Shall Find Her**	Irregulars, Holmes, Watson, Bella
10	**Vendetta**	Bella, Mrs Moriarty

ACT II

11	**Sherlock Holmes (Reprise)**	Irregulars, Mrs Hudson
12	**No Reason**	Holmes
13	**A Lousy Life (Reprise)**	Mrs Hudson
14	**My Incomparable Best**	Holmes
15	**Halcyon Days**	Watson, Martingdale
16	**Without Him, There Can Be No Me (Reprise)**	Bella
17	**London Is London (Reprise)**	Irregulars
18	**The Lord Abides in London**	Bella, Mrs Moriarty, Salvation Army, Irregulars
19	**Down the Apples 'n' Pears**	[Holmes], Bella, Company
20	**He's Back**	Irregulars, Company
21	**A Million Years Ago — Or Was It Yesterday?**	[Holmes], Bella
22	**A Million Years Ago — Or Was It Yesterday? (Reprise)**	Bella
23	**The Best of You, the Best of Me**	Holmes, Bella
24	**I Shall Find Her (Reprise)**	Holmes, Watson, Company
25	**Sherlock Holmes (Reprise)**	Full Company

SYNOPSIS OF SCENES

ACT I

ACT II

SYNOPSIS OF SCENES

ACT I

Spring, 1897

There is a bridge high across the stage. Below is a space where various rooms can be set: Baker Street, an artist's studio, etc. The stage pictures should be realistic, like the illustrations in the Strand Magazine. *The bridge, with steps up to it from the stage, becomes the bridge over the Reichenbach Falls, a bridge over a London street or the Thames, etc.*

Music 1: "Sherlock Holmes"

The CURTAIN *rises to the sound of wind and a towering waterfall. There is the stunning visual effect of a sheer rocky cliff face and crashing waters beyond a narrow ledge. Alone and lit on the ledge, Holmes stands in his deerstalker and ulster, confronting his arch-enemy, the master criminal Moriarty, at a range of only five or six paces. Their strong profiles are starkly silhouetted against the dramatic background. They shout over the thunderous roar of the raging waters*

Holmes So, Moriarty. The game is up!
Moriarty Whose game exactly, Holmes?
Holmes Yours, sir. Your life of crime!
Moriarty Without my life of crime, sir, your life of detection would have been singularly dull.
Holmes Don't trifle with me, Moriarty. You have no way out!
Moriarty Your way out's down there! In the Reichenbach Falls!
Holmes The world is like this ledge — too small to contain both of us!
Moriarty Then stand back! I shall clear my way! If I fall, you fall with me!

Holmes throws back his ulster and advances on Moriarty. Moriarty starts to open up a silver-knobbed cane to reveal a sword-stick, then changes his mind and throws the weapon aside, preferring to trust in the immense power of his large hands and long arms

The music (a dramatic variation on the main "Sherlock Holmes" theme) surges violently as the two great men grapple ferociously on the precarious precipice. The struggle and the music build to a terrifying climax as the two men totter on the brink of eternity, and finally fall. There is a high sustained violin tremolo, matched by the sound of two blood-curdling cries, as the two men fall, apparently to their deaths

   In the swirling mist, the figure of Watson is dimly visible

Watson *(calling out)* Holmes! *Holmes!* HOLMES!

The Lights fade, so that only the turbulent, foaming mists of the Reichenbach Falls are visible, which continue to swirl around the stage, and now magically transform themselves into the early morning mists and fog of London — specifically Victoria Station. The gate to Platform Ten appears slowly and dimly in the background, to the sound of trains and whistles and escaping steam and the slamming of carriage doors

The Lights come up on Victoria Station

   A scruffy group of lads (The Baker Street Irregulars) emerge through the mist. A couple of them are selling newspapers. The music changes mood: the same theme as before is transmuted now into a sad, minor key lament, as the lads stand downstage in stunned disbelief

Irregulars *(shouting out mournfully)* Sherlock 'Olmes dead! Tragic death of famous detective!

The newly-arrived boat-train from Dover disgorges the last of its passengers

   Among them is Dr Watson, wearing a black armband and looking heavy-hearted as he trudges out with two cumbersome suitcases, one of them bearing the initials S. H. He buys a newspaper and shakes his head as he looks at the headline

   A station porter approaches with a two-wheeled trolley. He has a broad West Country accent

Porter Come along now, sir. D'you wanna hand with them bags?

Watson, immersed in the newspaper, gratefully allows the porter to take his luggage

Watson Er — thank you, Porter. Yes, please.

Porter (*loading the bags*) That's a very bad business, sir, about poor Mr Sherlock 'Olmes.

Watson (*nodding gloomily*) In the fullness of time, Porter, it will be seen to be one of the truly great tragedies of our era.

Porter (*in Holmes's voice*) Like most retired Indian Army doctors, Watson, you have a particular gift for morbidly exaggerating the truth.

Watson drops his newspaper and looks at the Porter in utter amazement

Watson (*shaken*) Holmes! Is that *you*? It's not possible!

Holmes It *is* possible and it *is* I!

Watson Well, I'll be damned!

As Watson speaks, Holmes suddenly swings one of his suitcases into the air and pushes Watson sideways into a pile of luggage. At that precise moment a rifle shot rings out, followed by a blast on a police whistle and the sound of running footsteps. Holmes, completely unruffled, calmly helps Watson to his feet

Holmes Forgive me, Watson. As you looked up, I caught the glint of a rifle barrel up on the station roof reflected in your right spectacle. When news of Moriarty's death and mine reached London early today, I suspected that Colonel Moran, his number two, would seize the first opportunity of disposing of *you*, Watson. Since Moran is a superb marksman, when and where better, I thought, than your predictable arrival on the first available boat-train from Dover. Ah yes, here's the bullet! (*He examines a black hole in the centre of Watson's suitcase*) A Smith and Wesson blunt-nosed three-o-three — the same bullet he used to win Bisley in eighty-eight.

Watson (*nervously*) Shouldn't we perhaps lie low for a little longer, Holmes?

Holmes (*matter-of-factly*) He won't fire again. I sent anonymous instructions to Scotland Yard an hour ago. Even with the lamentable

Lestrade in charge, they will have apprehended Moran by now. As I thought. Look there, Watson.

Three grim-faced policemen escort a heavy-set, handcuffed man with red hair and moustache through the station concourse. A self-satisfied Lestrade brings up the rear. A shadowy figure — a woman dressed entirely in black — follows them at a distance, pausing to glance fleetingly at Holmes and Watson

Holmes looks at the shaken Watson with concern

My dear Watson, I owe you a thousand apologies. I had no idea you would be so affected. I've given you a serious shock, old fellow, by my unnecessarily dramatic reappearance.

Watson I'm all right, I assure you, Holmes, but I can hardly believe my eyes! You actually climbed out of that dreaded abyss? Doesn't seem possible! And what of that devil Moriarty?

Holmes Drowned in the Reichenbach Falls! I am sure of it! The end was terrible, Watson. He threw his long arms around me. We teetered together on the brink of the Falls. I applied the Slide of Cunning together with the Trip of Deceit from the Third Book of the Mystery of Baritsu.

He demonstrates the technique on Watson, sending him spinning once more into the pile of luggage. He steadies Watson

I beg your pardon, Watson.

Watson Not at all, old boy.

Holmes Over he went, dragging me with him. As we fell, I broke his grip — and saw him plunge into the raging waters below!

Watson Good God, Holmes! What a story! (*He removes his black armband*) Well, I shan't be needing *that* for a while! But I *could* use a rather severe drink. The shock, you know. What about the Café Royal?

Holmes If you'll forgive me, dear fellow, I'm hardly dressed for the Café Royal. I prefer your suggestion that we lie low for a while.

Watson Of course. Absolutely, Holmes. Selfish of me. Got a bit carried away, you know.

Holmes Understandably, Watson, understandably. I just need a little peace and quiet.

Watson Quite so.

Holmes A reflective pipe by the fireside ...

Watson (*a touch disappointed*) Exactly. That sort of thing ...

Holmes Maybe get some of the rust out of the old violin ...

Watson (*wincing*) Ah! *That* sort of thing ...

Holmes And if memory serves, Watson, there is a particularly fine magnum of eighteen forty-seven Château Lafite in the top left-hand corner of my wardrobe — a small token of esteem from the Maharajah of Jahore!

Watson (*beaming*) And a well-earned one! "The Mysterious Case of the Tiger's Eye." Welcome home, old fellow!

Holmes Come along, Watson — back to Baker Street! (*He turns away and opens the suitcase marked S. H. to change into his trademark ulster coat and deerstalker hat*)

Mrs Hudson (*off, calling*) Dr Watson!

Watson turns in surprise

Mrs Hudson, Holmes's landlady/housekeeper from 221B Baker Street, hurries in huffing and puffing, a tragic figure dressed from head to foot in black

Watson Mrs Hudson! What are *you* doing here?

Mrs Hudson (*dramatically*) I 'ad to come and meet you and console you ... an' meself! Oh, what a *terrible* tragedy! (*She bursts into floods of tears*)

Watson (*embarrassed*) Ah yes, well, you see, Mrs H. ... It's not quite as bad as you think ...

Mrs Hudson looks up as Holmes, now dressed as himself, turns back to face Watson and finds himself face-to-face with Mrs Hudson

Holmes (*smiling, breezily*) Afternoon, Mrs Hudson.

Mrs Hudson screams in horror and faints dead away into his arms

A simple curtsy would have sufficed.

Wiggins and a couple of Irregulars rally round and instantly recognize Holmes with roars of delight

Wiggins (*in amazement*) Mr 'Olmes! 'E's alive! 'Ere, lads! Look 'oo it is!

A crowd quickly gathers as Holmes is recognized amid general rejoicing. Mrs Hudson recovers instantly as the music surges, and the cheers redouble as Holmes is escorted triumphantly out of the station

The following song covers the journey back to 221B Baker Street

Song 1: Sherlock Holmes

Mrs Hudson	Sherlock 'Olmes
Watson	Is probably the greatest man alive!
Company	The greatest man of eighteen ninety-three
	Or four or five!
	The greatest man
	Of eighteen ninety-six or seven or eight!
	And other men with claims to fame
	Will simply 'ave to wait!
Wiggins	An' 'oo's the reason they will 'ave to wait?
All	Sherlock 'Olmes!
	Without a doubt the greatest man on earth!
Mrs Hudson	'E's so much more than anyone else
	That nobody knows 'is worth!
Watson	Success can only follow him,
	No matter where he roams —
All	The one an' only Sherlock 'Olmes!
Watson	The crisp and clinical,
	Slightly cynical
	Sherlock Holmes!
	Admittedly he has
	A somewhat liberal share of faults —
	The list is so appalling
	It could never be unfurled!
	But everyone's defective —
Mrs Hudson	Quite! And 'e is a great detective!
Wiggins	Quite the greatest in the 'istory of the world!

Watson	He has the intellect of the British Museum!
Wiggins	A mind as wide as the River Thames!
Watson	A brain as big as the Colosseum!
Mrs Hudson	An' eyes as bright as the finest gems!
Watson	It's from qualities such as these
	That Holmes's genius stems —
	And the masters of crime
	Have a miserable time
	With their tatty stratagems!
Company	And why?
	And why?
Watson ⎫	I'll tell you why!
Company ⎭	
Mrs Hudson ⎫	Sherlock 'Olmes
Company ⎭	Is certainly the greatest man there is!
	The great achievements of the day
	Are almost always 'is!
Mrs Hudson	An' I believe, in years to come,
	When memories grow dim,
	A lot of things 'e 'asn't done
	Will be ascribed to 'im!
Mrs Hudson ⎫	The greatest deeds will be ascribed to 'im!
Company ⎬	Without 'im, England's future would be grim!
Mrs Hudson ⎭	Sherlock 'Olmes
	Must surely be the genius of 'is day!
	When people finish speaking of 'im,
	They 'aven't a thing to say!
	An' one day 'e will take 'is place
	In 'istory's favourite tomes —
	The one and only Sherlock 'Olmes!
Watson	The egotistical, slightly mystical,
	Incorruptible, indestructible,
	One and only Sherlock 'Olmes!
Company	Sherlock 'Olmes!
	All said and done —
	Sherlock 'Olmes!
	There's only one —
	Sherlock 'Olmes!

They arrive at 221B Baker Street. Watson disappears into the house

Mrs Hudson pauses theatrically to acknowledge the plaudits of Holmes's admirers and then follows Watson into the house, slamming the door of 221B behind her

Black-out

SCENE 1

Holmes's rooms in Baker Street. Autumn 1897

There is the melancholy sound of a violin playing alone on the stage. (The tune is a mournful version of "Without Him, There Can Be No Me")

The Lights fade up slowly on the sitting-room, furnished as history knows 221B Baker Street: the table of chemical equipment, the two armchairs by the glowing fireplace, the pipe racks, books of reference, the confusion and mess, the coal scuttle in which Holmes keeps his tobacco. There are pistols, V.R. picked out in bullet holes on the wall, and a bust of Socrates with a clay pipe in his mouth. There is a sabre on the mantelpiece. Above a silver plaque fixed to the wall, in the place of honour above the fireplace, is displayed Moriarty's silver-knobbed sword-stick

Holmes looks appropriately sad as he plays the mournful melody. (Music: recorded violin.) An important-looking man in a frock-coat is standing with his back to the fireplace, his top hat, gloves and walking-stick on the table. He is greatly put out by Holmes's obvious lack of attention. He is Sir Jevons Jarndyce, Gentleman Usher of the Black Rod — the Court Official in charge of Parliament and the ceremonies of the House of Commons. He takes advantage of a pause in Holmes's violin playing

Jarndyce But Mr Holmes. I am here as the envoy of the entire House of
    Commons. As Gentleman Usher of the Black Rod.
Holmes I have already informed you clearly, Sir Jevons. I have been
    retired these several months, and intend to remain so. In any case, I can't
    feel that the theft of the mace from the Division Table of the House of
    Commons is going to make the honourable Members any more foolish
    or inarticulate than nature has already decreed ... (*He returns to the
    violin*)

Music: recorded violin of "Without Him, There Can Be No Me"

Jarndyce (*shouting over the violin*) But only you, sir ... could possibly solve such a mystery.
Holmes Nonsense. It is a routine enquiry. You should closely question any of your Members who may have a wooden leg.

The music stops. Holmes puts down the violin

Jarndyce Pray why, sir?
Holmes Because the Speaker's mace is not an object easily concealed in a top hat! You must think more of things like tool bags, folded stretchers, bass fiddle cases, coffins, cricket bags, golf bags — all highly suitable mace transporters!
Jarndyce (*deeply impressed*) You *amaze* me, Mr Holmes!
Holmes (*pulling a bell rope*) Now Sir Jevons, I must ask you not to interrupt my retirement further ...
Jarndyce (*collecting his top hat, gloves and cane; pausing*) Mr Holmes, is there no man alive who could tempt you back to your profession?

Holmes goes to the mantelpiece and picks up a long leather instrument case

Holmes (*thoughtfully*) Only one man.
Jarndyce Perhaps, if the Prime Minister ...
Holmes In my view, the Prime Minister could only tempt people *into* retirement — hardly to emerge *from* it! (*He picks up Moriarty's sword-stick*) But if a certain obscure professor of mathematics ... no chance of that, however ... he is no longer alive!

Mrs Hudson knocks and enters

I must ask you, sir ... to leave me now to the long silence of my private thoughts. Mrs Hudson. You will show Sir Jevons out. (*He opens the instrument case, which contains a syringe*)

Mrs Hudson leads Jarndyce out

Mrs Hudson (*whispering sympathetically*) No luck, sir?

Jarndyce I must confess I couldn't raise a flicker of interest.

Mrs Hudson I'm afraid nothing seems to interest 'im, now 'e's retired.

Mrs Hudson and Jarndyce exit

At the sound of footsteps mounting the staircase, Holmes puts the open instrument case on a side table and lolls back in his chair, his eyes closed

Watson comes bustling in. He looks at Holmes, who doesn't open his eyes

Watson (*genially*) Evenin', Holmes. (*He moves across to the fireplace, warming his hands*) Holmes ... wasn't that Sir Jevons Jarndyce I passed on the stairs?

Holmes Yes, the mace has disappeared from the House of Commons and they sent me Black Rod. A singularly gloomy old stick.

Watson (*turning to him, shocked*) My old friend! Resorting to puns? (*He sees the syringe in the open instrument case*)

Holmes What else do I have to while away these empty years?

Watson (*picking up the syringe*) It seems you *do* have something else. Something of which you know that I disapprove heartily.

Holmes Dear old Watson! You have no conception of the depths of depression a man can suffer ——

Watson Indeed I have, Holmes ... when the wind is easterly, I still have the damnedest trouble from that old Jezail bullet the murderous Ghazis lodged into me during the Second Afghan War. At such moments I treat myself to a Turkish bath and a stiff whisky! I don't turn myself into a pincushion!

Holmes picks up the violin and plays another mournful few bars of "Without Him, There Can Be No Me". (Music: recorded violin) Watson thoughtfully puts the syringe back into the case. He winces at a bad note from the violin

Watson You might consider giving *that* up, too!

Holmes (*putting down the violin*) I tell you, doctor, London has become a singularly uninteresting city since the death of the late lamented Professor Moriarty! (*He displays Moriarty's sword-stick, pulling out*

the dagger) This grim memento is all that remains of him. (*Admiringly*)
I tell you, Watson, there were no stratagems like *his* stratagems.
Watson Holmes! You rid society of its greatest enemy!

Music: introduction of "Without Him, There Can Be No Me"

Holmes And rid myself of the one foeman worthy of my steel.
Watson (*reprovingly*) Oh, come now, Holmes — stuff and nonsense!
Your genius for solving the unsolvable is legendary! I mean ...

Holmes lapses into even deeper gloom

Song 2: Without Him, There Can Be No Me

Watson	You're speaking of the man Who solved "The Boscombe Valley Mystery".
Holmes	(*bored*) Well, that's history!
Watson	And "The Scandal in Bohemia" —
Holmes	Than which nothing could be seamier!
Watson	And "The Red-headed League" —
Holmes	A pathetic intrigue!

Holmes yawns. Watson tries again

Watson	The man who solved the riddle of "The Engineer's Thumb" —
Holmes	The mere memory makes me numb!
Watson	"The Solitary Cyclist" —
Holmes	Is on my "do-not-like" list!
Watson	"The Yellow Face" —
Holmes	A dreary case!
Watson	"The Sign of Four" —
Holmes	God, what a bore!
Watson	"The Crooked Man" —
Holmes	A puny plan!
Watson	"Wisteria Lodge" —
Holmes	A dismal dodge!
Watson	Well, what about "The Adventure of the Dying Detective"?

Holmes	(*showing his first glimmer of interest*) Now there, my
	friend, perhaps
	You're getting slightly more selective!
Watson	"The Case of Lady Carfax" —
Holmes	(*nodding*) That *did* have some bizarre facts!
Watson	"The Abbey Grange" —
Holmes	Yes, that was strange!
Watson	"Black Peter" —
	And "The Naval Treaty", too!
Holmes	(*smiling*) I must confess, Dear Watson,
	The simplistic list of plots
	On which you base my reputation
	Proves it's true!

Watson (*puzzled*) What is?

Holmes That I am missing Moriarty.

Watson (*shocked*) Missing that *fiend* Moriarty?

Holmes Without the perfect criminal, Watson, there can *be* no perfect detective!

> Without fire, there can be no flame!
> Without players, there can be no game!
> Without Shakespeare, there'd be no "To be or not to be"!
> Without him, there can be no me!

Watson Oh, come now, Holmes — I think you're rather over-estimatin' the feller!

Holmes By no means, Watson.

> Without day, there can be no night!
> Without wrong, there can be no right!
> Without evil, there can be no good of great degree!
> Without him, there can be no me!

Watson Rubbish! Your achievements are second to none, Holmes — even *excluding* your encounters with Moriarty!

Holmes David fought many battles, Watson, but it is for Goliath that he is remembered.

> Without light, no dark —
> Without Noah, no ark —
> Without him, no spark
> To relieve my gloom!
> Without hope, no chance —
> Without Paris, no France —
> Without him, no romance
> In life, I assume!

Watson seems devastated by his revelations

Don't you see, Watson, Moriarty and I were totally interdependent! One simply doesn't *exist* without the other!

The music builds

> Without love, there can be no hate!
> Good and ill both decide our fate!
> Without him, no mystery
> To which I am the key!
> Without him, no moments
> Only he can guarantee!
>
> So all in all, as far as I can see,
> Without him, there can be no me!

As the song ends, Holmes takes a revolver from the pipe-rack and places one bullet in the chamber. He raises the revolver, fires it across the room, and the clay pipe falls shattered from Socrates' mouth

Watson (*protesting*) Holmes! Marriage may have its drawbacks, but at least we don't have revolvers in the drawing-room.

Holmes On the contrary — the Sunday newspapers persuade me that revolvers in the drawing-room are a constant feature of British marriage. It's the only way men can have the last word! (*He throws himself down into his chair again*)

Watson looks out of the window

The truth is, Watson, I am *bored*! I have more than enough money to
retire — but less than enough interest to work ——

Watson (*turning back into the room, excited*) Very well, then, Holmes!
I *challenge* you! A wager! (*He consults his half-hunter watch*) It is now
two minutes to four! I'll bet you the best dinner that Simpsons-in-the-
Strand can offer that you cannot unearth the missing House of Commons
mace by six o'clock this evening!

Holmes (*stifling a yawn*) Tempting wager, old man, but ——

Watson (*with huge enthusiasm*) Good fellow!

Mrs Hudson enters carrying a letter which she hands to Holmes

Mrs Hudson Letter for you, sir.

Holmes takes the letter, glances at it, and sniffs

Holmes (*matter-of-factly*) Delivered by hand by a red-headed fishmonger.

Mrs Hudson (*gaping*) Yes, sir. How d'you know?

Holmes (*shrugging*) No stamp, reeks of fish, and here (*he extracts a hair*)
is the red hair. Thank you, Mrs Hudson. (*He opens the envelope
dramatically with a deft flick of the savage-looking sabre from the
fireplace*)

Mrs Hudson (*wincing and withdrawing*) Yes, sir. (*She mutters to herself*)
'E does 'ave some funny ways.

She exits

*From the envelope Holmes draws a single playing card. He stares at it,
transfixed for a moment, then flings off his dressing-gown and grabs his
ulster and his deerstalker from the hat rack by the door*

The underscore begins

Holmes (*urgently*) Come, Watson. A good brisk walk will work wonders
for your Jezail bullet.

Watson Good idea, Holmes. Er — where are we going?

Holmes (*handing him the playing card*) Look at that and *tell* me, Watson!

Watson (*studying the card*) The ace of diamonds ... er — game of cards?
You want to play bridge at Crockford's.

Holmes Try again, Watson. Look more closely. The upper lines of the diamond have been produced downwards, forming, for anyone who cares to observe it, the letter M. (*He calls*) Mrs Hudson, our coats, if you please! (*Significantly*) M, Watson!

Watson (*blankly*) Ah, yes, M. Jolly good. As in Mother!

Holmes (*with mounting excitement*) And M plus ace most certainly means mace! Diamonds mean Hatton Garden ... (*he turns the card over*) On the back, a fish motif — and that means Billingsgate! Well done, Watson!

Watson (*baffled*) Not at all. Pleasure.

Holmes I hope you booked that delicious dinner at Simpsons!

Holmes hurries out of the room, afire with enthusiasm

Watson (*complaining*) But Holmes — you haven't won the bet yet!

He scurries out after Holmes

Outside 221B, Holmes is already deep in conference with the two principal Irregulars, Wiggins and Mossop. They listen intently to his urgent whispered instructions, nodding their comprehension

Holmes ... and let me know if you see any suspicious characters carrying large objects.

Wiggins Consider it done, Mr 'Olmes.

Holmes Excellent. Come along, Watson.

Watson What was all that about?

Holmes No clues, Watson. This is a wager.

He propels Watson away as the music builds. The following song covers the Irregulars' journey to Billingsgate Fish Market

Song 3: Anything You Want to Know

Irregulars	Fer you, Mr 'Olmes,
(variously)	There ain't nuffin'
	The Irregulars 'ere wouldn't do!
	'Cos we know
	You got great faith in us,

Mr 'Olmes —
Like yer know
We got great faith in you!

Send us 'ere —
Send us there —
Send us any ole where —
The Irreg'lars yer know'll come through!
Gettin' full confirmation
Of all information
'Bout what, which, where, 'ow, when an' who!
'Ow, when an' who!

If there is
Anything you want to know —
Just think of
Anything you want to know —
There must be
Something that you want to know —
And if there is, well,
'Tis well —
I know where to go.

Wiggins   The price of a barrel of biscuits,
Or slices of veal and ham pie,
The place to buy cherries,
Or dry Spanish sherries,
These are examples —
A few random samples —
Of merchandise I can supply.

Irregulars   If there is
Anything you want to know —
If there is
Anywhere you want to go —
There must be
Somewhere that you want to go —
And if there should be,
Could be,
I'm the man to know.

Mossop A tour of the Tower of London,
A look at the works of Big Ben,
A cruise to Bermuda,
Or p'raps something ruder,
You just decide it
And I will provide it
With one dazzlin' stroke of me pen.

Irregulars If there is
Anything you want to see —
If there's a door
To which you need a key —
I'll take you
Anywhere you want to be —
Just take my 'and, mate,
And, mate,
Intimate to me.

They arrive in Billingsgate

SCENE 2

Billingsgate Fish Market

The song builds to a climax as the Irregulars arrive

Wiggins A sniff around Billingsgate Market —
A whiff o' the world's freshest fish!

They sniff in unison, then pull appalled faces at the stench

Irregulars Cor!
Wiggins The odour o' kippers
From Great Yarmouth skippers —
Smells that provide ways
Of knockin' yer sideways —
With any fish dish that you wish!

Irregulars	If you seek
	Any sorta fishy treat,
	This 'ere's
	A very fishy sorta street!
	We'll sort out
	Any fish you want to eat!

Wiggins	When you're with me,
	You'll see the Billingsgate elite!
Irregulars	An' find out
	Anything you want to know!
	Anything you want to know!
	Anything you want to know!

Holmes and Watson have arrived at a Fishmonger's stall, which bears the legend "Bert Briggs — The Best in Billingsgate"

The Irregulars spot Holmes and Watson and hasten to join them

Holmes Well, Wiggins, did you find out anything I want to know?

Wiggins (*embarrassed*) Er — 'fraid not, sir, no! We was busy ...

Holmes No matter, no matter ...

Watson (*triumphantly consulting his half-hunter watch*) It's two minutes to six, Holmes!

The Fishmonger holds up a large salmon

Holmes What do you say, Watson? Would you like to take home a salmon for Mrs Watson? To make up for staying late at the club last night, keeping dinner waiting and then saying you weren't hungry.

Watson (*amazed*) Holmes! How can you possibly know that?

Holmes The smear of billiard chalk on your left cuff, and on your right the unmistakable stain of the club's steak and kidney pudding!

Watson (*rubbing his cuff, guiltily*) Well, nobody's perfect!

Holmes Two minutes to six, eh? (*To the Fishmonger*) A nobler piece than that tiddler, man! Let me see now ... (*he points to the sack under the barrow*) What have you got in that sack down there?

Fishmonger (*pulling out the sack*) 'Ow's that fer a whopper, sir? This fish is so fresh, it swam up the Thames to Tower Bridge, caught a number twelve bus an' got 'ere about two minutes afore you did!

A roar of laughter from the other fishmongers

Holmes Shall we inspect this monster of the deep?

A crowd gathers round. Holmes suddenly plunges his arm into the sack and pulls out a glittering and golden object. As he does so, a police whistle sounds

A good catch, wouldn't you say, doctor?
Watson (*amazed*) The mace! (*He looks at his watch*) I'll be damned! Thirty seconds to spare!

Holmes hold up the mace triumphantly. The crowd presses round

Inspector Lestrade forces his way through the crowd with two policemen

Holmes The mace it is, Watson! And here comes Lestrade to tell us it has every appearance of stolen property!
Lestrade Here! That has every appearance of stolen property! (*He breaks off and stares at Holmes*) Well, well, well — Mr Sherlock Holmes!
Holmes Well, well, well — the late Inspector Lestrade! Here. Return this bauble to the House of Commons. It seems our elected spokesmen are tongue-tied without it ...
Lestrade Constable, take charge of this evidence.

He signals to a Constable, who takes the mace from Holmes

Holmes, I thought you were retired.
Holmes Just trying to set you a good example, Lestrade.
Lestrade (*deciding this is a compliment*) Me? Oh no, sir. No, I don't retire for many more years yet! And both my sons have joined the Force.
Holmes (*wincing*) We are doubly blessed, Watson! Another generation of Lestrades!
Lestrade What puzzles me, Mr Holmes ——
Holmes (*affectionately*) Wouldn't it be simpler to tell me what *doesn't* puzzle you, Lestrade?

Lestrade (*ignoring the slight*) — is how you knew where to retrieve the mace!

Watson Yes, Holmes, explain to him how you knew it was in that particular sack!

Holmes There were no more than four obvious reasons. You noticed them, of course, Watson.

Watson (*taken aback*) Me? Er — not really *four*, no.

Lestrade (*shaking his head*) It looks just like any other sack to me ... what else was there to *see*?

As Holmes describes and clarifies each of the four points, Watson says, "Ah yes, of course!*", and the crowd oohs and ahs and ums and ohs at each revelation*

Holmes First, the sack was made of Japanese imported jute, unobtainable in Britain. Second, the knot was a German Reefer, as distinct from the more usual Billingsgate Bowline. Third, the faint stamp of the Swiss customs officials was still discernible ... and fourth, when the stallkeeper accidentally struck it with his boot, I heard a loud clang! (*He turns to Lestrade in reflected triumph*)

Watson (*proudly*) Elementary, my dear Lestrade!

Lestrade Well, not much more scope here, sir, for your powers of detection. Right, let's get the darbies on this one!

A policeman clicks handcuffs on the protesting Fishmonger

Fishmonger 'Ere! Wot you doin'? I ain't done nuffin'!

Lestrade is moving off with the arrested Fishmonger when Holmes stops him

Holmes Lestrade! You obviously have lost none of your flair ——

Lestrade Thank you, sir.

Holmes — for doing the wrong thing! (*He turns to Watson, talking quietly, but with great suppressed excitement*) It takes the thickness of a Lestrade, Watson, to imagine that a man would steal the mace of the House of Commons, then seek to dispose of it among a flurry of flounders and take the trouble to inform *me* of its whereabouts ... No!

There are hints of deep waters here, Watson ... deeper, I fancy, than we have gazed into since we saw the depths of the Falls of Reichenbach!

Holmes and Watson stroll off together, deep in conversation. As they depart, The Woman in Black detaches herself from the crowd, watches them for a moment, then disappears again in the swirl of people

Song 3a: Anything You Want to Know (Reprise)

Wiggins

> A peep at Sir Samuel Pepys's diary —
> A run round the 'ouse o' Nell Gwynn —
> The second you spot it —
> You name it — you got it!
> From Buckingham Palace
> To my Auntie Alice,
> There's no door that I can't get in!

Irregulars

> I'll take you
> Anywhere you want to be —
> I'll show you
> Anything you want to see —
> I'll tell you
> Anything you want to know
> So if there is, well,
> 'Tis well —
> Simply tell me so!
>
> I'll tell you
> Anything you want to know!
> Anything you want to know!
> Anything you want to know!

The Lights cross-fade to:

SCENE 3

Holmes's rooms in Baker Street

Holmes, sitting in his fireside chair, his face buried in a book, is looking amused and unusually cheerful while Watson listens to a beautifully dressed lady, the Duchess of Monmouth, who is pacing the room in acute distress

Duchess I will be revenged, gentlemen — on the fiend who kidnapped my darling Reggie!

Watson (*taking notes*) Your Grace was telling me of his daily routines and habits ...

Duchess Yes, Reggie never rose before ten. He liked to walk across the park from Belgravia at eleven-thirty sharp — and we would drop in at the Ritz for a quarter bottle of Moët-Chandon.

Watson (*nodding approvingly*) Very civilized. Thirsty work, walkin' across a park!

Duchess For luncheon, when we didn't have guests, he preferred Claridge's. A wing of partridge, washed down with a saucerful of Romanée Conti. The seventy-four.

Watson (*writing*) The seventy-four. Excellent. (*He looks up, frowning*) A saucerful? (*Confused*) Forgive me. Your Grace, Reggie is ——

Holmes (*without looking up*) Her Grace's King Charles spaniel, Watson.

Watson (*stunned*) King Charles *spaniel*? You mean, he's a *dog*?

Duchess You don't think I'd be seen at Claridge's with my *husband*, do you? The Duke of Monmouth's way of drinking soup is not something that should be inflicted on the general public!

Holmes gets to his feet, laughing softly

(*Coldly*) I'm sorry you find my personal tragedy so amusing, Mr Holmes.

Holmes It's simply, Your Grace, that you are the fourth Duchess in twenty-four hours who has consulted me about a lost King Charles spaniel! (*He picks up a list from the mantelpiece*) Their Graces of Richmond, Tyneside, Argyll ... and now Monmouth ... (*he writes it on the list*) who have been mysteriously deprived of Gerald, Vernon, Norman ... and now ...

All Reggie!

Duchess (*on the brink of tears*) Oh, Mr Holmes, will you take the case? I have heard of your retirement.

Holmes (*very seriously*) Four Duchesses ... Four King Charles spaniels ... yes, Your Grace, your problem interests me strangely.

Duchess (*emotionally*) Thank you, Mr Holmes. My future happiness is in your hands.

Holmes Then it is quite safe, madam.

The Duchess sweeps out of the room

Watson bows low. Holmes inclines his head, then rubs his hands in glee

Watson (*grumbling*) I must say, old boy, you might've *told* me Reggie was a King Charles spaniel! I felt a bit of a ninny!
Holmes (*animated*) Don't you *see*, Watson? It's another signal!
Watson Damned if I can see any signals.

Holmes studies his list of names. Suddenly, a smile spreads across his face and he snaps his fingers

Holmes Of course! I've got it! As before, it has the genius of breath-taking simplicity. Just let me put them in the right order for you — look at this, Watson — after the mace of diamonds, we now have the four ladies! Monmouth, Richmond, Argyll and Tyneside. Got it?
Watson (*firmly*) No.
Holmes (*patiently*) Write down the first two letters of each of their names.
Watson (*spelling the letters out cumbersomely*) Monmouth ... M. O., Richmond ... R. I., Argyll ... A. R., Tyneside ... T. Y., Mo-ri-ar-ty. Good God! Holmes! It spells *Moriarty*!
Holmes (*clapping him on the shoulder*) Well done, Watson! I knew you'd spot it! We also have four kings!
Watson (*repeating the process*) Reggie ...
Holmes Vernon, Norman and Gerald — which, applying the same principle ——
Watson Reggie ... R. E., Vernon ... V. E., ...
Holmes (*cutting in*) *Revenge*, Watson! There's no doubt about it — the game is well and truly afoot! Our old occupation has returned, and that heavy tread upon the stair, unless I very much mistake it, is Inspector Lestrade, come to tell us that he has had to let Briggs the Fishmonger go.

Lestrade enters

Lestrade (*puzzled*) I've had to let Briggs the Fishmonger go ...
Holmes Well, what a surprise! Of course, there's no possible case against him ...

Lestrade He says that a bag of fish was sold to him by a stranger he met at Billingsgate — a tall, thin fellow with piercing eyes — gave his name as Mr Uriah Clid.

Holmes (*with a short burst of laughter*) Uriah Clid — ha! ... The devil's very own sense of humour! No doubt he used his initial. Uriah thus becomes ...

Watson U ... Clid?

Holmes Exactly! Your ingenuity astounds me, Watson. Euclid. Author of *The Elements of Geometry*. The man who discovered the relationship between pyramids and prisms. An apt pseudonym, wouldn't you say, for the second greatest mathematician in the history of the world?

Watson Holmes. You cannot mean ——

Holmes Yes, Watson — Moriarty is well and truly back among us. Indestructible as myself!

The underscore begins

Watson But at the Reichenbach Falls ...

Holmes The body was never discovered, remember? Those long arms. The man was a powerful swimmer.

Lestrade Mr Holmes!

Holmes Out of your depth, Lestrade?

Lestrade Just assuming he's back, why would he want to steal the mace of the House of Commons and ——

Watson Serve it up on a fish slab!

Holmes For the same reason he stole four King Charles spaniels from four of the most doting, dog-loving duchesses in the land! To announce his presence, gentlemen! An act of defiance entirely in the character of Professor James Moriarty! (*He starts to pace the room. From the place of honour above the fireplace he removes Moriarty's silver-knobbed sword-stick, which he flourishes as he strides up and down*)

There is a knock at the door

Mrs Hudson enters with a card on a salver

Watson takes the card and looks at it. He nods to Mrs Hudson

Mrs Hudson leaves the room

Watson (*handing the card to Holmes*) It's for you, Holmes. An invitation to this evening's private view at the Royal Academy ...

Holmes (*reading the back of the card*) A personal note from a Miss Bella Spellgrove ——

Watson How do you know that?

Holmes — it's on the back — begging us to attend, for a reason she cannot divulge in a postal communication!

Watson Sounds a bit mysterious.

Holmes (*examining the card*) It raises several interesting questions.

Lestrade Such as why she asked you ...

Holmes (*handing Lestrade the card*) Such as why she was in such a tearing hurry to get to the post, how the invalid in her family is getting on, why she should trouble to conceal her continental upbringing ... and whether her contribution to this year's Academy is being hung. Of course all these questions will have already occurred to you.

Lestrade gives the card back to Watson, who stares at it blankly

Watson (*waffling*) Er ... well, er ... one or two, perhaps.

Holmes Of course, Watson! You know my methods. We must concentrate upon details!

Lestrade (*opening his notebook*) What details?

Holmes sighs patiently. Throughout the following song Watson stares blankly at the invitation

Song 4: Look Around You

Holmes　　　　In my life as in my work, Watson,
　　　　　　　　I have always found
　　　　　　　　That it pays to keep an ear,
　　　　　　　　As they say, to the ground.

Watson Quite so, Holmes.

Holmes　　　　A depressing fact of life, Watson —
　　　　　　　　Terrible but true —
　　　　　　　　Is that if you notice nothing,
　　　　　　　　Nothing notices you.

Watson I hadn't noticed.
Lestrade Nor me, neither!

Holmes   No, precisely!
                   But from here on in
                   I recommend that you do!

Lestrade Do what?
Holmes Look around you, Lestrade!
Lestrade What for?

Holmes sighs again. It is an uphill struggle

Holmes   Many minor miracles surround you —

Watson Do they really?

Holmes   How do you detect what they might be?

Watson I've no idea!

Holmes   All you have to do is look around you —

Lestrade Where?

Holmes   Just look around you —

Lestrade I'm looking.

Holmes   And you'll see!

Watson I'm damned if I can see anything! (*He looks out of the window*)
    Ah yes, there's a bus!
Holmes But what *number* bus, Watson?
Watson (*baffled*) Oh ... er ...
Holmes It's a number two to Neasden! You see.

                   There is mystery *everywhere* around you!

Watson You're not serious.

Holmes   Easy to unravel if you try.

Lestrade I've never really thought about it.

Holmes   Sometimes the solutions will astound you.

Watson You don't say!

Holmes   Just look around you —

Lestrade I'm looking.

Holmes   And ask why!

Lestrade Why what?

Holmes   Well, I mean why do flowers have a million hues —
Making the world a perfumed kaleidoscope?

Watson I haven't the faintest idea!

Holmes   They are blue, and yellow, and vermilion clues —
Telling us the world has hope!

Watson   How nice to have a world with hope!

Holmes Absolutely, Watson!

Never let your fears and doubts confound you!

Watson and Lestrade examine the invitation, equally baffled

Watson Of course not!

Holmes   Things are better than they might appear.

Watson I'm sure they must be!

Holmes   Don't forget that miracles surround you —

Watson I won't!

Holmes   Just look around you —

Watson I will!

Holmes   And it's clear!

Lestrade ⎱ (*together*) What is?
Watson ⎰

Holmes   That on the whole it's good to be here!

Lestrade I wonder.
Watson Holmes, all these little details you ... we ... noticed about this invitation. Explain them to ... er ... Lestrade here.
Holmes (*showing Lestrade the card*) Certainly, I mean ...

First, the stamp —
The stamp is stuck on upside down —

Watson (*nodding at Lestrade*) Haste!

Holmes   (*sniffing the card*) Second, I detect a medicinal aroma, I think.

Watson (*nodding at Lestrade*) Invalid!

Holmes   (*pointing at the card*) And then third, her misuse of the abstract noun ——

Lestrade (*frowning*) What's an abstract noun?
Watson (*pointing vaguely at the invitation*) There's one in there. Shows she's *foreign*.

Holmes   And fourth, she writes in black squid ink! Very *rare*!

Watson (*to Lestrade*) Holmes wrote a monograph on ink!
Holmes Only artists use it!
Watson (*triumphantly to Lestrade*) She's an artist! Mrs Hudson, our coats, please!

Holmes   Come on, Watson!
                    Never let your fears and doubts confound you!
Watson ⎱   Never let your fears and doubts confound you!
Lestrade ⎰

Holmes   Things are better than they might appear.
Watson ⎱   Things are better than they might appear.
Lestrade ⎰
Holmes   Don't forget that miracles surround you.

Watson I won't!

Lestrade   Just look around you!

Watson I will!

Holmes   And it's clear ——

Watson ⎱ (*together*) Er — *what* is?
Lestrade ⎰
Holmes (*exasperated*) Oh, for God's sake, man!

> That on the whole it's good to be here! (*He suddenly twists the handle of Moriarty's sword-stick and draws out its glittering dagger*)

Lestrade I'd suggest you put that away, Mr Holmes. We don't want you getting into any trouble ...

Holmes Don't worry, Lestrade. On the day my arch-enemy declares himself to be back in our midst, it won't be Sherlock Holmes that finds himself in trouble!

All   Yes, on the whole it's good to be here!

Holmes snaps the blade back into the sword-stick

The Lights fade

SCENE 4

The Royal Academy

Music: an up-tempo, pizzicato variation on the theme of "Look Around You" as the Lights cross-fade to reveal a tableau of a fashionable late-Victorian crowd in toppers and huge hats and parasols

*Behind them the set reveals a wall of pictures at the Royal Academy. The
people move to look at the paintings. A banner announces the exhibition
to be one of "Contemporary European Artists". Nearby is a recess,
screened from the main gallery by potted ferns. There is a gallery seat in
the recess. On the wall, number twenty-three is an empty frame, from
which the canvas has been jaggedly cut out. Bella is sitting on the seat in
front of it in deep dejection*

Holmes and Watson enter. Watson is reading a catalogue

Watson Anything here you'd recommend, Holmes?

Holmes (*glancing round*) Yes, I'd say twenty guineas for those sunflowers
by Van Gogh is probably a sound investment, Watson ... and I'd also
take a shot on that sixteen-year-old prodigy from Spain — young
Picasso!

Watson (*doubting*) Mm ... Twenty guineas is a lot of money. I know
where you can buy *real* sunflowers for a penny each! Ah, here we are!
Number twenty-three, "Portrait of a Stranger", by Miss Bella Spellgrove.

Holmes Come then, Watson. Let us find number twenty-three ...

Watson notices Bella and is instantly devastated by her beauty

Watson (*nudging Holmes*) My God, Holmes, look at that gorgeous
woman!

Holmes Miss Bella Spellgrove, I take it.

Bella (*looking up at him and smiling sadly*) Thank heavens you've come,
Mr Holmes. What I feared most has happened ...

Holmes (*glancing at the wall*) The rather brutal removal of your picture ...
When did this happen?

Bella It was found to be missing when the Academy opened for the
viewing.

Watson (*devotedly*) I am *totally* at your service, madam! You are in no
other danger, I trust?

Bella (*taken aback; smiling*) Thank you. No, none.

*Holmes quickly examines the frame and the remnants of the canvas,
making lightning calculations as he does so*

Holmes The thief was six foot two, wore black shoes, and had a badly sprained right wrist. He was in a great hurry, and used a blunt kitchen knife. Can you describe your portrait, Miss Spellgrove?

Bella A man's face ...

Holmes Any particular man?

Bella I met him at a small pension in Switzerland. A strangely solitary man — but fascinating to draw — such piercing eyes, and a high, dome-like forehead.

Holmes (*intrigued*) He sat for you?

Bella (*shaking her head*) I drew him secretly — from a distance. He used to sit alone for hours, reading some dull, boring book of mathematics ...

Watson Mathematics.

Holmes And when was this painting done?

A couple of art lovers wander into the recess to view the paintings

Bella Just a few weeks ago.

Holmes A few *weeks*? (*To himself*) So it is possible! Er — Watson. Have you any of those foul Indian cheroots about you? Those you learnt to smoke on the North West Frontier?

Watson (*beaming*) My Khyber Clouds, you mean? Of course! Always carry stacks of 'em! Takes me back to ——

Holmes (*cutting in*) Light one up, there's a good fellow. We must not be interrupted, and one puff of a Khyber Cloud will most certainly ensure our total privacy.

Watson takes out a cheroot and lights it

At the first puff, the art lovers start to cough and splutter, and instantly leave the trio alone

Describe the man further, Miss Spellgrove ... if indeed you can tolerate this disgusting smoke-screen!

Watson (*with excessive gallantry*) I wouldn't *dream* of inconveniencing Miss Spellgrove ...

Holmes Go, Watson! Puff!

Watson goes, rather sulkily, to the entrance of the recess and blows out smoke while Holmes and Bella talk rapidly

Passers-by quicken their pace, start coughing and give them an extremely wide berth

Bella He was a little older than yourself. Very tall. With singularly long arms ...

Holmes Did you by any chance see the title of the book he was reading?

Bella (*nodding*) He left it on the hallway table one day. It was called *The Dynamics of an Asteroid*.

Holmes (*with a sharp intake of breath*) Then it's *true!*

Watson turns to look at him, puzzled

He has arisen from the dead! A feat only two of us have ever achieved ... myself and Moriarty.

Watson I say, Holmes! Steady on!

Holmes Well, I grant you, there may be certain biblical parallels. Miss Spellgrove, I must inform you that the man you painted is a genius of crime — the greatest in history — who would go to immense lengths to steal any portrait of him ... *and* destroy its creator!

Watson But surely, Holmes, if Moriarty is indeed alive — and advertising his presence — would he object to having his portrait exhibited?

Holmes He would object to having his *identity* revealed! We are in deeper waters now, Watson! Not merely paddling ...

Bella I'm deeply concerned by what you say, Mr Holmes. Ever since I came to this country I have had the distinct impression of someone following me ...

Watson That doesn't surprise me in the *least!*

A man strays into the recess

Holmes Go and puff, Watson. Nearer the entrance please, and with the prevailing wind, preferably.

Watson puffs like a steam train

The man promptly chokes and staggers away, clutching his throat

Holmes (*to Bella*) You don't live in this country?

Bella (*shaking her head*) No, I come from Lucerne. In Switzerland. This is my first visit to London.

Holmes And you are caring for an invalid ... someone close to you?

Bella No. I'm sorry, Mr Holmes. I have no family, and all my friends are in rude health.

Holmes (*frowning*) But my methods ——

Watson (*pleased*) Are not infallible, apparently.

Holmes One thing is abundantly clear, Miss Spellgrove. You are in particular peril.

Bella (*smiling enigmatically*) I do believe I am.

Holmes You have seen his face.

Bella (*mysteriously*) I have indeed ... seen his face.

Holmes turns to Watson as Bella walks away to look at the paintings

Holmes Watson. A word with you. We must remove this young lady to a place of safety ——

Watson (*with great enthusiasm*) What a splendid idea, Holmes!

Holmes You have a spare bedroom.

Watson (*his face falls*) Oh, no! Impossible, Holmes!

Holmes (*puzzled*) But surely, Mrs Watson is reasonable enough.

Watson Mary is a brick, of course ... but if I took home a beauty like Bella Spellgrove, I fear the domestic upheaval would far outstrip the horrors of the Second Afghan War ...

Holmes Then there is nothing for it. Mrs Hudson must prepare the box room. She can be passed off as my landlady's cousin. Over from the continent.

Watson (*astonished*) Holmes! You mean you would accept ... female company?

Holmes In an emergency, Watson, one is obliged to make certain sacrifices. (*He crosses to Bella*) Miss Spellgrove, I cannot offer you any particularly lavish hospitality ...

An Attendant enters and approaches Watson

Attendant (*coughing*) Excuse me, sir. There's been a complaint made, on the subject of your smoking.

Holmes (*turning away from Bella*) Stamp out the foul mundungus, Watson. We are going to Baker Street. (*He emits a bizarre, high-pitched whistle*)

Wiggins instantly enters

Wiggins, you will escort Miss Bella Spellgrove to 221B, but she must not be seen to enter the house.

Wiggins (*his eyes shining at the prospect*) Consider it done, Mr 'Olmes.

Watson (*to Bella, gallantly*) I would consider it an honour and a privilege ... (*he offers his arm*)

Holmes (*taking Watson's proffered arm*) Come, Watson. We have much to do.

Watson But, Holmes — Miss Spellgrove ...

Holmes propels the protesting doctor firmly away. As they leave, the mysterious Woman in Black appears fleetingly on the far side of the gallery, watches them for a moment, and disappears

Wiggins repeats Holmes's high-pitched whistle

The other Irregulars magically materialize and surround Bella. She surveys her scruffy escort with amusement

Bella So are you going to show me London?

Wiggins (*in disbelief*) You mean you've never been 'ere before? *Really*?

Bella Why should I have?

Mossop Greatest city on God's earth, miss.

Bella Have you seen Paris?

Wiggins (*dismissing it out-of-hand*) Don't 'ave to, do we?

Bella How about Rome? Or Venice?

Mossop (*with disdain*) Nah! Full o' foreigners, i'n't they?

Bella Then why London?

Wiggins Well, because ... I mean, it's *London*, i'n'it?

Song 5: London Is London

Wiggins   Eros stands in Piccadilly Circus
                            Nelson stands in Trafalgar Square
                            Big Ben stands by the River Thames,
                            And will as long the Thames is there.
                            London is a strange, unchanging town,
                            And take my word —

Whatever you've 'eard —
London Bridge 'as no intention
Of falling down.

Irregulars London is London,
Is anyone in doubt about it?
London is London,
It's easy to find out about it.
London is springtime —
Cockney champagne.
London is summer —
Lots of rain,
But who's complaining?

The song continues as the Lights cross-fade to:

SCENE 5

The Streets of London

The Irregulars give Bella their colourful guided tour of "The Greatest City on God's Earth" as the set changes to reveal the streets of London. They show her the low life as well as the high life as they make their way to 221B Baker Street. Bella becomes almost unrecognizably overdressed to look like one of the Irregulars during the following

Irregulars London is lovely —
Let no-one change 'is mind about it —
Lovely and lively —
Yes, that's the thing I find about it.
You can 'ave Paris an' Venice an' Rome —
But London is London
Is London
Is England
Is 'ome!

All London is London —
Forgive me if I shout about it.
Nowhere's like London,

So why be roundabout about it?
London is history,
Future and past.
London is mystery —
Flabbergasting!
Everlasting!
It's the bleedin'
Garden of Eden!

London's a charmer —
I could go on for days about it!
Drippin' with drama —
There just ain't no two ways about it!
You can 'ave Cairo an' Cannes an' Capri —
An' anywhere else that you're 'appy to be!
But London is London
Is London
Is England
Is me!

The music builds. The key lifts and the tempo slows

An' London is somehow
The only place I wanna be in
London can somehow
Make every man a 'uman bein'.
Wiggins   Bein' in London
One 'as to take heed!
Mossop   'Cos villains abound
An' are bound to succeed!
All   But London is London —
An' London is all that I need!

Bella and the Irregulars arrive at 221B. Wiggins rings the doorbell

Mrs Hudson appears

Mrs Hudson (*suspiciously*) What you up to, Wiggins?
Wiggins (*sweetly*) Personal message from Mr 'Olmes, mum!

He draws her conspiratorially a few feet away from the front door

In a flash, the Irregulars slip Bella into the house unseen. Holmes and Watson enter

Wiggins nods to Holmes, then rejoins his group

Holmes (*genially*) Ah, Mrs Hudson! A word.

They exit into the house together, followed by Watson. The door closes

The Irregulars gather near the door, listening intently

Wiggins I'd say about five seconds. One ... two ... three ... four ——

Mrs Hudson's ear-splitting scream sends the delighted Irregulars running gleefully for cover

Mrs Hudson (*off*) A woman in the 'ouse!

Song 5a: London Is London (Reprise)

Irregulars   But London is London —
                    An' London is all that I need!

SCENE 6

Holmes's rooms in Baker Street

The rooms have been tidied up and dusted. Papers have been neatly put away. We now see chintz curtains and cushion covers: everything is bright and sparkling. A kettle is steaming on the hob. By the fire is a tray with a whisky decanter, sugar and lemon

Bella is arranging flowers on the table in the middle of the room. Watson sits in Holmes's chair, ostensibly reading The Times, *glancing constantly across the room with a sigh at the divine Bella*

Bella leaves the room

The music for "Her Face" begins

Watson Oh, my God!

Song 6: Her Face

I am a man
Who has travelled down the years
With considerable regard for the ladies.
Now I have a wife,
But elsewhere in my life
There were Jennifers and Hildegardes
And Sadies.

I flatter myself
That in one or two things
I am something of a connoisseur.
One of those things is women,
But of all the lovely women
I have seen
I have never seen
The likes of Bella Spellgrove.
No, I've never seen
The likes of her ...
Her face ... her face ...

*Unnoticed by Watson, Mrs Hudson enters the room with a feather
duster*

*As she starts to flick things clean in his vicinity, she overhears his words
and reacts to them as though they were intended for her*

I don't think
I have ever seen
Anything lovelier than her face.
Her look is a little exclusive,
Her nose just a little obtrusive,
Her manner a little elusive,
A trace.

But her face
Has a magical mystery
Memory can't erase.
Her smile is alive and amusing,
Her beauty a little bemusing,
And I am in heaven perusing
Her lovely face.

Bella returns with more flowers

*Watson is immediately aware of her presence, but still doesn't notice Mrs
Hudson is in the room. Mrs Hudson very slowly becomes aware of the
reality of the situation, and glares at Bella with ill-concealed jealousy and
loathing*

A face beyond any endeavour
A pleasure to treasure forever
A miracle nothing could ever
Replace.

The doorbell rings

(*Speaking; imperiously*) Mrs Hudson. The doorbell.

*Mrs Hudson exits in high dudgeon. Bella follows her out, devastating
Watson with a smile*

What I feel
When those wonderful eyes of hers
Hold me in their embrace
Is something for poets to pray to —
For beautiful music to play to —
But something I never could say to
Her face ... Her face ...

(*Simpering*) I don't think
I have ever seen
Anything lovelier ...
Than her face.
(*He sighs deeply*) Her face!

As he goes to leave the room, he bumps into Bella re-entering

(*Covered in confusion*) Ah, Miss Doorbell! There's someone at the Spellgrove ... I mean ... er ... oh, dear ...

As he exits, consumed with embarrassment, Watson gallantly hands Bella a small posy, like a bouquet, from the flowers she had been arranging at Holmes's desk

Bella hears footsteps approaching the door. She opens it and steps back in alarm

Confronting her is a frightening-looking, bent, wizened old man wearing black-lensed spectacles, carrying a tray of watches and tapping a white cane as he ventures into the room

Bella Who are you?
Blind Man (*in a rich Donegal brogue, urgent and excited*) Blind Ben O'Hara, miss — wid important news for Mr Sherlock Holmes! An' you — wi' that sweet, gentle voice like the laughter of angels — you mus' be that lovely young Miss Bella, what's secretly stayin' here!

Bella, recovered from the momentary shock, doesn't blink an eye. She responds immediately with cool-as-a-cucumber, quick-thinking astuteness

Bella Indeed I am. But since Mr Sherlock Holmes would most certainly never allow any such secret to be divulged, Mr O'Hara, and since he is also reputed to be a master of disguise, I can only assume that *that* is who you are! Would you like a cup of tea, Mr Holmes? Or perhaps a hot toddy. (*She turns back into the room without so much as a backward glance*)

Holmes, furious and somewhat deflated by her coolness, starts to remove his disguise

Holmes (*disgruntled*) Hot toddy.
Bella (*helping him into his dressing-gown*) Your disguise and your accent were really quite good.

Holmes (*acidly*) Don't patronize me, Miss Spellgrove! (*Intrigued*) How did you know it was me?

Bella (*pointing at his feet*) That v-shaped tear in the toe-cap of your left shoe. I noticed it when I cleaned it this morning.

Holmes (*with grudging admiration*) Very impressive! Splendid! You sound almost like me!

Bella (*with an edge*) High praise indeed! Just how many of you *are* there?

Holmes Many disguises, of course — this blind watch-seller, for example, is so successful that I have seriously considered giving up detection to do it full time. But in fact there is only *one* Sherlock Holmes ... despite appearances. (*He drops into an armchair*)

Bella kneels by the fire and prepares the hot toddy. Holmes finds a pipe and puts it in his mouth. Bella looks up at him sympathetically from the fireside

Bella So why the elaborate disguise?

Holmes I have been searching for signs of our mutual enemy.

Bella And you found nothing?

Holmes Nothing as yet! This is a three-pipe problem ... Where is my tobacco?

Bella (*reaching for it*) It's here. Ready-rubbed Empire mixture. Very good.

Holmes (*surprised*) How did you know?

Bella I recognized the aroma and the texture when I tidied up.

Holmes Very perceptive. (*Testily*) I don't *like* being tidied up, Miss Spellgrove. On second thoughts, I'll have a cigar.

Bella obediently replaces the slipper and returns to him with the coal scuttle, opening the lid for him. Holmes watches her like a hawk

Why is the coal scuttle over there by the window? I like it over *here* by the fire!

Bella (*matter-of-factly*) By the fire is too hot. Over there by the window it maintains a constant sixty-two point five degrees Fahrenheit ... which is the ideal temperature for your Cubas. They'll last longer and smoke better that way. I attached a thermometer inside the lid for you, so you'll know in future.

As she speaks, she chooses a cigar for him, rolls it between thumb and forefinger against her ear, clips it expertly, lights it and hands it to him. Holmes, impressed, is for once at a total loss for words

I also cleaned them ...

Holmes Miss Spellgrove! I never smoke clean cigars! In future I suggest you confine your destructive talents to the box room! (*He paces the room testily*) There was a pile of white powder on this table.

Bella (*firmly*) You don't need cocaine, Mr Holmes! I therefore thought it better to throw it away!

Holmes (*furiously*) You *thought*! You *thought*! You task is not to *think* anything! Your task is to sit still and permit me to save you from the clutches of the resurrected professor!

Bella Perhaps ... I'm used to being more active, sir.

Holmes sinks back in the armchair and sticks his feet out to the fire

Holmes There is no earthly need for women to be *active*! As soon as they drop their needlepoint they get into immediate trouble.

Bella (*with spirit*) A woman brings both beauty and peace into a man's life, Mr Holmes.

Holmes (*with heavy sarcasm*) The most beautiful woman I ever saw poisoned her three children for the insurance money. When action is called for, Miss Spellgrove, women are at their best confined to a darkened room, with a slight nervous headache ...

Bella (*standing her ground*) Well, *I'm not*! So I bought some flowers to brighten up *this* room instead! (*She pours out a whisky toddy*)

Holmes They'll all be killed by my chemical experiments. Don't tell me! You've tidied up those as well!

Bella One superior hot whisky toddy! (*She hands the steaming glass to Holmes with a dazzling smile*)

Holmes Who taught you to make a hot whisky toddy?

Bella My mother used to make them for my father. You know, you are a uniquely interesting man, Mr Holmes. One day I should like to do a portrait of you.

Holmes I have no desire to sit for a portrait, Miss Spellgrove, I wish to *remain* a uniquely interesting man. (*He relents*) You know, this toddy's not at all bad.

Bella (*pointedly*) Don't patronize me, Mr Holmes. Actually, that is the first sign of your behaving like a normal human being.

Holmes (*sipping the toddy*) And *this* is the first sign of your becoming a fellow lodger fit to be mentioned in the same breath as the great Doctor Watson ...

He sips the drink, almost approvingly, as soothing music begins

Bella But *he's* not a woman.

Holmes Of all Doctor Watson's many qualifications as a near-perfect companion, *that* is the foremost!

Bella But is he pretty? Is he fragrant?

Holmes *Watson?* Of course he is! He's as pretty as a walrus, and as fragrant as a Khyber Cloud! But with all his faults, he's ... he's *Watson!*

Bella *Ha!*

Holmes (*raising his eyebrows*) What do you mean, ha?

Song 7: Men Like You

Bella	How typical — how typical!
	Hiding behind such a feeble excuse —
	(*Scornfully*) "He's Watson!"
	Such a lovable goose!
	Who's only held in high regard
	Because he flatters your façade!
Holmes	(*stunned by the onslaught*) Façade?
Bella	(*dismissing the interruption*) A typically arrogant
	masculine attitude!
	Highly sensitive!
	Full of ingratitude!
	Because you are frightened of women,
	Your friends are all wet!
	There's no intellectual stimulus,
	Challenge or threat
	To endanger the small-minded,
	Self-serving rules that you set!
	You set your sights low —
	And low's what you get!

Holmes (*speaking; from a great height*) Miss Spellgrove, I ...

Bella   (*ignoring him*) How totally, totally typical of the frail
                             male set!

Holmes (*speaking; interjecting*) Miss Spellgrove ...

Bella   Men like you
                             Infuriate women like me
                             Because you're too stubborn to see
                             That women are such intelligent
                             Elegant creatures!

                             Men like you
                             Exasperate women like me
                             Because you prefer us to be
                             Subservient fools
                             All drooling for masculine teachers!

                             Small surprise
                             You see such sadness in our eyes —
                             Men just don't realize
                             The harm they do!
Holmes   Me!?
Bella   I mean, men like you —
                             You aggravate women like me,
                             Devaluate permanently
                             Our point of view.
                             And that is why, you see —
                             It's tragic, but it's true —
                             That women like me
                             Like battling men like you!

Holmes (*speaking*) I suspect there is more to you than meets the eye, Miss
Spellgrove, but that tirade was a heart-rending piece of propaganda,
totally lacking in any evidence to support it!
Bella (*speaking*) Look around you, Mr Holmes!

Holmes   It's typical! Quite typical!
                Failing to make any logical sense,
                Attack is your devious means of defence!

                Your views, which reason can't conceive,
                Don't even flatter to deceive!

Bella (*speaking*) Mr Holmes ...

Holmes   A typically dangerous feminine attitude,
                Lightweight in intellect,
                Heavy in platititude!

                You say I am frightened of women —
                Well, *that* I must doubt! —
                For one simple reason,
                What could I be frightened *about*?

Bella (*speaking; wickedly*) Shall I tell you?

Holmes   (*backing off*) My friends, you imply,
                Offer no intellectual threat —
                In fairness, they *try* ——
                (*With a small smile*) — but they haven't as yet!

Bella (*speaking*) The *arrogance* of the man!

Holmes   For you to attack them
                Is typical of the she-male set!

Bella (*speaking; outraged*) *She*-male!?

Holmes   (*nodding*) *She*-male!
                Women like you,
                You seem to hate men like me,
                The reason is tricky to see —
                Since women are such a delightful,
                Unspiteful species!

Bella (*speaking; still outraged*) *She*-male!?

Holmes	A lady like you,
	How could she hate men *en masse*?
	Which might appear clumsy and crass,
	Were men not charmed and disarmed
	By the harm she unleashes!

Such a shame
Angels by any other name
Should slander and defame
The way they do!

Bella Me?

Holmes I mean, women like you,
You underrate men like me,
You overstate violently
Your point of view!
The simple truth is this —
For all the world to see —
That women like you
Like *challenging* men like me!

They pace the room in opposite directions, outwardly seething, each of them simultaneously annoyed with and intrigued by the other, and yet enjoying the confrontation

Women like that
Quite fascinate men like me,
Creating quite ominously
Conditions that Watson's sure
To say there is no cure for!

Bella Men like that
Infatuate women like me,
And generate gen'rally
Emotions that somehow
One should be sure to insure for!

Holmes	Even though
	It's just a moment's mood,
Both	I know ...
	I like it even so ...
	So ... What to do?

With simultaneous resolve:

	No!
Holmes	Women like ...
Bella	Men like ...
Both	That can devastate
Holmes	Men like ...
Bella	Women like ...
Both	Me —
	Which indicates clearly
	That we
	Should leave it be ...
	And that is why, you see —
	It's tragic, but it's true —
	That
Holmes	Men like me like ...
Bella	Women like me like ...
Holmes	Staying well away from ...
Bella	Running in dismay from ...
Holmes	Women like ...
Bella	Men like ...
Both	You!

They both storm out of the room

The Lights fade and come up downstage where we can see the front door of 221B Baker Street

Scene 7

Outside 221B Baker Street

A bored and shivering Potatoes Clark, on guard duty outside 221B, blows on his hands to warm them

A sad-looking Mrs Hudson, still clearly humiliated by her recent encounter with Watson and Bella in Holmes's study, enters from the house

Potatoes looks up, sees her and seizes his opportunity

Potatoes Just goin' ter get meself a cup of 'ot broth — OK, Mrs H? Back in a minute. Must be nice for Mr Holmes to have a woman in the 'ouse at last!

He dashes off

Mrs Hudson seethes and starts polishing the brass numberplate of 221B furiously. Music begins: the Vendetta *underscore*

Behind Mrs Hudson, the shadowy figure of The Woman in Black steps into a nearby doorway, looks at the upper windows of 221B, and blows two blasts on a strange-sounding reed instrument

A hand waves down from the upper window

The Woman in Black disappears as swiftly as she came

Mrs Hudson looks round in surprise. Suddenly she stops her polishing and emits a huge sob

Song 8: A Lousy Life

Mrs Hudson   Good fortune in this world
                   Is seldom evenly spread!
                   So said my 'usband Fred,
                   An' the next day 'e was dead!

An' since that day,
In early spring of eighteen sixty-three,
Fred 'Udson's diabolical luck
'As all rubbed off on me!

Can you imagine
Bein' a bride
On the first of May —
An' widowed on the seventh?!

Can you imagine
Thinkin' you're rich
On the followin' day —
An' broke by the eleventh?!

Can you imagine
Learnin' the day
Before your dear 'usband's funeral
"'Ey, the doctor is glad ter say
'E thinks you just may
Be 'avin' a baby!"

It 'appened ter me,
All o' them things —
They 'appened ter me,
By the time I was twenty-three!
As a woman —
As a widow —
As a wonderful,
Would-be, worthy wife,
Mine
'As been a lousy life!

Holmes, with his pipe firmly in place and his ulster collar pulled up so that his face is barely visible, hurries out of the house and sets off down the street

A musical pang as Mrs Hudson gazes after him devotedly. As she turns back, "Holmes" looks quickly around, just long enough for us to realize that it is in fact Bella in disguise

Bella exits

Mornin', sir!
Can you imagine
Me the grand lady
Of Baker Street?
Well, that's 'ow I'm regarded!

(*Snobbishly*) When you are
Sherlock 'Olmes's landlady
You *make* a street!
That's why I keep 'im guarded!

Can you imagine —
'Im bein' single —
Given 'ow lodgers
An' landladies mingle —
My passionate tingle
Rejected?!
The one thing 'e's *not* detected! (*She shakes her head in despair*)

It 'appened ter me,
All o' them things,
They 'appened ter me —
'Ere I am now at —— (*her wavering hand indicates "give-or-take-a-bit"*)
— Forty-three!

What a gory
End-of-story!
In an 'ouse 'old
Where romance should be rife!

Mine 'as been a tragic —
Sorta short on magic —
Truly lousy life!

Music continues under as Watson emerges from the house in a bowler hat and overcoat

Mrs Hudson regards him with slightly hurt adoration

Watson (*breezily*) Mornin', Mrs Hudson.
Mrs Hudson Mornin', sir. Where you off to so bright an' early?
Watson (*gleefully confiding in her*) Thought I'd just nip down to the
corner sweet-shop an' get Miss Bella a nice box of chocolates. Small
token of esteem, eh? You know how it is!

He winks and wanders off with a dreamy, faraway look in his eyes

The twice-scorned Mrs Hudson bridles with rage and frustration

Mrs Hudson (*bitterly*) There's no fool ——

—— Like an old fool!

The music builds

Can you imagine
'Avin' yer eye on
A lovely man —
Since eighteen eighty-seven?

Can you imagine
Bidin' yer time
With a long-term plan —
Anticipatin' 'eaven?

An' then imagine
Some brazen 'ussy —
Forward, flirtatious,
An' clearly not fussy —
Lures 'im becuss 'e's so stupid
'E acts like a love-sick Cupid!

It 'appens ter me —
Only ter me —
The things that yer see!
If I live ter be ninety-three,

I am fated
Ter be frustrated!
Can me 'eart stand
The endless stress an' strife?

Mine 'as been a gallin',
Awful an' appallin',
Tot'lly unenthrallin',
In need of overhaulin',
Truly lousy life!

Suddenly there is a mighty shout from within the house

Holmes (*off*) She's *gone*! Watson! Wiggins! Mrs Hudson!

*A distraught Holmes emerges and joins Mrs Hudson at the door of 221B
as Watson returns, bearing a large box of chocolates, and the Irregulars
hurriedly assemble*

Mrs Hudson She can't 'ave done! I'd 'ave seen 'er!

Watson (*shocked and concerned*) Bella? ... *Gone*?

Potatoes Gone *where*, sir?

Holmes A woman just doesn't disappear into thin air, Mrs Hudson!
You're quite sure no-one left the house this morning?

Mrs Hudson *Quite* sure, Mr 'Olmes. *No-one* except yourself, sir — an'
Doctor Watson.

Holmes Watson, we *have* to find her! If I lose her, I lose all possible
contact with Moriarty! Wiggins, Mossop, lads, Miss Spellgrove has
disappeared. Are you with me, lads?

Wiggins }
Mossop } (*as one*) Yes, sir!

Holmes Then *find* her!

Wiggins But where do we look, Mr 'Olmes?

Holmes If I read that young lady aright, Wiggins, anywhere and
everywhere!

The pulse of the music intensifies

Song 9: I Shall Find Her

Mossop	Somewhere in the 'eart of London —
Wiggins	Some dumb 'umdrum slum of London —
Irregulars	Somewhere there's a beautiful girl
	A needle in an 'aystack —
	A diamond in a dustbin —
	Sunlight in a cold grey sky —
Holmes	And somehow I shall find her —
Irregulars	(*echo repeat*) Find 'er — find 'er — find 'er —
All	By and by ...
Holmes	Where in God's name in this city
	Is this gritty demoiselle?
	In the grip of Moriarty —
	Come to drag her down to hell?
	'Tisn't easy to protect her,
	For I like her far too well!
	Where in London do I find this wayward belle?
Irregulars	Somewhere, somehow,
	I shall find her ...

The Lights cross-fade to:

SCENE 8

The Streets of London

The set changes into a maze of London streets and alleyways as the search party sets out through the swirling mists of low-life London, seeking the elusive Bella. From time to time we glimpse her, now dressed in a hooded black cloak, flitting through the foggy, gas-lit streets, confusing and compounding the searchers' task

The Irregulars spread the word of the search among their many seedy-looking friends and contacts in the seamier side of London society

Company	By a statue ... by a river ...
	By a fountain ... or by chance ...

                    At a wedding ... at a funeral ...
                    At a party ... at a glance ...
                    In a tramcar ... in a taxi ...
                    In a tantrum ... in a trance ...
                    Somewhere, somehow, I shall find her ...
Wiggins   (*exasperated*) What a dance!

   Come on!

The Irregulars race off after him

Watson   (*romantically*) By a love-seat, by an elm tree,
                    By a millhouse by a stream,
                    In a dungeon in a castle,
                    In a moment in a dream ...
Holmes   I have no way of predicting
                    When or where we're meant to meet —
                    On a Monday ... on a Tuesday ...
                    On a corner of a street.
Watson   (*daydreaming*) But there's one thing that is certain —
                    That the moment will be sweet —
Irregulars   Somewhere, somehow, I shall find her —
                    I repeat ...
                    And when I find her, this I know —
                    I shall never, never ever let her go!

                    I shall find her ...
                    I shall find her ...

As everybody searches, Bella appears unobserved on the bridge above them

Unaware of her proximity, they continue singing in counterpoint to her

Bella   He will find me — when I let him —
                    Let him search down every street!
                    When I'm ready, I will get him!
                    And it's more than me he'll meet!

He will also meet disaster!
My revenge will be complete!
Any moment I'll apply my sweet deceit!

*Wiggins catches a glimpse of Bella in her black cloak as she slips away.
He looks the other way and sees The Woman in Black disappearing in
the opposite direction*

The Irregulars give chase to both

Holmes	Will I find her in a minute?
Watson	(*still dreamy*) Will I find her in an hour?
	In a moment filled with sunshine —
	Or a rainy April shower?
Wiggins	In the tea-leaves in my teacup?
Mossop	In the petals of a flower?
Holmes	Somewhere, somehow, I shall find her —
	Give me power!
Company	In a huddle in a doorway ...
	In a downpour in a storm ...
	By a fireside roasting chestnuts,
	Where it's cosy, where it's warm ...
Irregulars	By her manner, by her beauty ...
	By her sweetness, by her size ...
Holmes	By her costume, by her perfume ...
Watson	(*enraptured*) By the colour of her eyes ...
Company	What a moment!! What a victory!
	What a triumph! What a prize!
	Somewhere, somehow, I shall find her —
	Somewhere, somehow, I shall find her!
	By surprise!

The music builds

*Bella reappears, undoes a locket from her neck and deliberately drops
it down from the bridge. It lands at Wiggins's feet*

Wiggins looks up quickly

Bella disappears

Wiggins Mr 'Olmes!

*Holmes hurries over as Wiggins picks up the locket and hands it to him.
He looks up to the bridge where Wiggins is pointing*

Company   And when I find her, this I know —
                   I shall never, never, ever let her go!

There is a big dramatic vocal finish

   Holmes strides purposefully off after Bella

*The Lights fade to Black-out. The music segués to the sinister "Vendetta"
theme*

SCENE 9

Bella's studio. Night

The Lights fade up as the "Vendetta" theme continues

*There is a skylight in the high ceiling — the opening of the skylight is on
a level with the bridge above the stage. There are two tall easels in the
centre of the studio — the canvases on the easels are turned away from us.
There is a stove on which are standing a kettle and a whisky bottle, etc.
There is a door* UC. *Holmes's deerstalker and coat hang on a hook nearby.
On a model's platform there is a throne-like chair, behind the chair a
curtain covering an alcove. There is a table of paints and brushes, and
canvases sloped against the wall. The studio is lit with gas lamps*

*Bella is standing and painting. She moves to the mantelpiece, strikes a
match and lights a stick of incense, which starts to smoke gently. She
smiles, watches the incense for a moment, then moves to the door. She
quickly turns a key in the lock, then moves to the second easel and starts
sketching. She hears a sound, and presses back against the wall*

*Holmes picks the locks, silently opens the door and enters. He carries
Moriarty's sword-stick*

Bella (*stepping forward*) Mr Holmes, what a pleasant surprise! I am truly flattered that you went to such trouble to find me.

Holmes stands, looking at her curiously as she closes the door

Holmes You are obviously unhurt ...
Bella (*still smiling*) Quite unhurt.
Holmes (*handing over the locket*) Yours, I believe.
Bella I am afraid I have been guilty of a terrible deception.
Holmes I am afraid you have. (*He notices the deerstalker and coat*) So *that's* how you left the house!
Bella (*moving away towards the stove*) Since the day we met, I have been determined to paint your likeness. That noble forehead! Those eyes burning like coals ... It's a picture I knew I *must* do. Can you understand my obsession?
Holmes Oh yes, I can *understand* it! I just don't *believe* it!
Bella I knew when I asked you in Baker Street you would never consent to sit for me ...
Holmes Quite so. Pray go on. My whereabouts may change when I *leave* Baker Street, Miss Spellgrove — but *not* my opinions.
Bella (*seductively*) I thought, if I lured you to my studio, you might change your mind.
Holmes Did you now?
Bella It was wicked of me.
Holmes It was deceitful of you. I am aware that both qualities are highly regarded by women like you.
Bella You are angry?
Holmes I am curious. And I *still* don't believe you!
Bella (*pouring out a hot whisky*) One hour. In that chair. With one of my hot whisky toddies. Does that sound so terrible? (*She holds out the glass to him with a disarming smile*)
Holmes They say every man has his price. Clearly this is mine. (*He takes the hot toddy from her, examines the chair suspiciously and finally sits in it with a smile. He sips and finishes the drink while they talk*) Now, Miss Spellgrove, male to she-male, do you mean to say that you went to these extraordinary lengths ... *just* to get me to sit for a *portrait*?
Bella (*with a sly humour*) Artists are ruthless people, Mr Holmes. You'd be *amazed* what I would do to get what I want!

Holmes Now *that* I *do* believe! (*He sniffs*) You're burning a very obscure incense ... it's Burmese! (*He sniffs again*) "Rangoon Rhapsody", if my memory serves me.

Bella (*smiling and nodding*) Very good, Mr Holmes! I find it gives my sitters a feeling of pleasure and relaxation. Now ... turn your head a little.

Holmes You are in the business of turning heads a little, I fancy.

Bella Now I have that magnificent profile against the light.

We hear an operatic female voice sing a couple of lines of "Vendetta" off-stage. The music continues under the rest of the scene. Bella sings a couple of lines as though in reply

Holmes (*seeming very relaxed, almost tired*) Mystery upon mystery! The first act duet from Cressubi's *Vendetta*. One seldom hears it!

Bella (*carelessly*) Oh, it's that mad Italian opera singer. She has a studio here — she never stops rehearsing. (*She picks up her palette and starts to work quickly on the canvas*) Like that. The brows drawn together in thought. Admirable! Yours is a face of infinite mystery, Mr Holmes. You must have secrets no-one can guess.

Holmes Speak for yourself. I'll tell you. After Reichenbach there seemed no crime worthy of my serious attention. I decided to retire. I was bored.

Bella I can't imagine you would tolerate retirement or boredom easily.

Holmes (*his voice sounding strange, drugged*) I didn't, until there were hints ... small, subtle, humorous — like clever schoolgirl pranks — until your case assured me that the Great Criminal was indeed *alive* after all!

Bella Are you sure of that?

Holmes You should know. You have drawn his face.

Bella I have drawn *both* your faces. The likeness is extraordinary ... but *which* is the Great Criminal?

Holmes (*trying to loosen his collar, seeming too weak to do so*) It's hot in here ... the stove ...

Bella The one whose eyes are merciless ... whose high forehead has room for every thought — except human understanding ...

Holmes (*sleepily*) Moriarty ...

Bella I'm talking about *you*, Mr Holmes! (*She turns the easel*) Though the similarities *are* striking! (*She draws aside a curtain, revealing several sketches of Moriarty hanging on the wall*) Look!

She shows him the missing portrait of Moriarty. The portraits of Holmes and Moriarty are stunningly alike

Holmes (*looking intensely into Bella's eyes*) The similarities are indeed striking. Of course, the eyes ... (*He tries to stand, but he is overcome with weakness. He slumps back in the chair, hardly able to speak*) It's that confounded incense!

Bella lays down her palette. She moves towards Holmes, who loses consciousness

Bella It's not the incense. It's the drink. The hot toddy. Oh no ... it won't kill you, Mr Holmes. Your death will be much more original. I think it will appeal to your sense of style. You hounded a man to his destruction — just for your entertainment! Did you enjoy hunting my father, Mr Holmes? Was it enough to save you from boredom? I can promise you — you will be bored no longer!

She looks at him. His eyes are shut, and he is drugged and helpless

I'm sorry. I shall have to finish your portrait ... from memory. No more children's games, like stolen maces and King Charles spaniels, Mr Holmes! *This* game is for grown-ups — and we play to the death! (*She turns the gas lamps right down*)

The stage is almost entirely dark. In the darkness the "Vendetta" music swells. Bella opens the studio door

We dimly see the now familiar Woman in Black holding the dead body of a girl in her arms — a girl who looks and is dressed like Bella

Mrs Moriarty Come, Bella.
Bella (*softly*) Yes, Mama.

Mrs Moriarty carries the dead girl over to the easel and with Bella's help, lays her carefully on the ground. Bella kneels beside the body, visibly moved

Poor darling Maria ... (*She looks up at her mother*) What a terrible end!
Mrs Moriarty Do not mourn for your sister, Bella. Rather give thanks to the illness that took her. In death she can do what no Moriarty has done in life — destroy Sherlock Holmes! (*She crosses to Holmes, spits at him,*

then removes the dagger from Moriarty's sword-stick) This is the moment when your father will finally be avenged. Come, Bella, take the sword. (*She proffers it*)

Bella (*hesitating*) Mother, I ...

Mrs Moriarty (*commandingly*) Take it! Remember your promise, Bella ... Repeat it.

Bella's hands clasp the handle of the dagger as the resolve returns to her eyes

Bella (*nodding; reassuring herself*) Sherlock Holmes must die!

Mrs Moriarty (*soothingly*) The plan was yours, child ... Brilliant like your father.

Bella His brilliance is safe in me, Mama.

Mrs Moriarty (*prompting her*) Not only death for the murderer Holmes, you said ...

Bella (*as though reciting*) ... but a disgrace equal to that he inflicted on the memory of my father. (*She looks into her mother's face, now totally determined*) Death *and* disgrace, Mama. Believe me, he shall have them *both*!

The music builds, underscored by a sinister Gregorian chant sung by an unseen chorus. The following song is sung around the unconscious Holmes, suggesting a pagan death ritual, with the Moriarty dagger seemingly destined to end Holmes's life

Song 10: Vendetta

Bella   Death — disgrace —
                     Will smile like skeletons
                     In his face —
                     Death — disgrace —
                     The just rewards
                     Of Holmes's last case.
                     And at the end,
                     No friends at his side —
                     Dogs have died better —
                     Vendetta!
                     Vendetta!
                     Vendetta!

Mrs Moriarty One man
      We will wait for —
      Whom we hold
      Untold hate for!
      That man's
      Days are numbered —
      Clearly numbered!
      Death unencumbered
      We will bring to him —
      Grim as Brothers Grimm—
      Tear him limb from limb
      At our whim!

Bella Sherlock Holmes will die!
Die a death
That money can't buy!
We will make his torment linger!
We won't lift a single finger!
We will see his spirit crumble —
Eating humble pie!

Mrs Moriarty That man will die!
God, how he'll die!
That wretched worm —
We will watch him squirm!
The dog will die!
Oh, how he'll die!

Mrs Moriarty Come, Bella, for your father. (*She unsheathes the sword-stick blade*)

Bella Death — disgrace —
Will hold him
In their chilling embrace!
Damn his name —
Extinguishing
His flicker of fame —
And Lady Trust
Is ashes and dust!
If she cries,
Let her!
Vendetta!
Vendetta!
Vendetta!

Mrs Moriarty One man
We shall cherish —

Until we
See him perish!

That day
We'll remember —
We'll dismember
Every ember
Of his memory —
For the world to see
That day will be so sweet for me!

Chorus voices continue under the following dialogue

Mrs Moriarty holds the blade high and grasps Bella's hand

Mrs Moriarty Now, Bella! *Now!*
Bella (*backing away in horror*) No!
Mrs Moriarty Call yourself a Moriarty? You're a weakling! (*She plunges the dagger downwards into her dead daughter's body*) There! It's done! Holmes is a dead man!

Bella Sherlock Holmes will die!	**Mrs Moriarty** Revenge is sweet!
I demand an eye for an eye!	So nice and neat!
He who kills a Moriarty	And Holmes's defeat —
Best prepare his funeral party!	It will be complete!
Don't rely on any past good	No fond goodbyes
At the last goodbye!	The day he dies!

Both   Sherlock Holmes will die!
                Vendetta! Vendetta! Vendetta!

Mrs Moriarty gets to her feet, embraces Bella, and silently leaves the room, leaving the stunned Bella holding the blood-stained dagger

Bella stares at it in horror for a long moment, transfixed, then goes into action

She wipes the handle of the dagger clean and places it firmly in the hand of the unconscious Holmes. She crosses to the door and carefully turns the key in the lock. She looks around the room, smiles at the drugged figure of Holmes and signals up to the skylight window. It promptly opens and Mrs Moriarty lowers a ladder. Bella climbs up till she reaches the skylight

She climbs out on to the roof (which is the bridge), pulls up the ladder after her and exits

The music stops. There is a violent knocking at the studio door

Lestrade (*off*) Open up! Open up there!

Holmes stirs. He gets up and moves to the body lying in front of the easel. The knocking continues

Open up or we'll have this door down. I'm warning you!

Holmes stoops down by the body, then looks at the blood-stained sword-stick dagger in his hand

Open up in the name of the law!

Holmes stands and turns towards the door as it's broken open

   Lestrade rushes in followed by a crowd of policemen whose bullseye lanterns light up the room

The policemen turn up the gas lamps. The stage is suddenly brilliantly illuminated — and the picture is of a murderer caught in the act. A dead girl with Bella's clothes and hair of her colour is lying in front of the easel. Holmes is standing holding the dagger from his own sword-stick. The easel has been turned round so we see the unfinished portrait of Holmes — who has been discovered alone with a corpse in a locked room

The Policemen take hold of Sherlock Holmes and snap the handcuffs on his wrists. Lestrade's and Holmes's eyes meet. Tableau

CURTAIN

ACT II
SCENE 1

Bella's studio

The entr'acte music segués into a reprise of the chilling Gothic vocal chorus of "Vendetta" as the Curtain *rises. The setting is the same as it was at the end of Act I, except that the body has been removed — an outline of where it lay has been chalked on the floor*

PCs Tomkins and Bottomley, at the door, hold a cluster of onlookers at bay. Lestrade, with enormous self-satisfaction, is walking around the studio making notes. He wears a long scarf. Holmes is sitting on the model's throne smoking his pipe, apparently still drugged and lethargic, actually watching Lestrade's movements sharply. He is handcuffed to the throne by his right hand

Lestrade (*looking at the broken indoor lock and making a note*) Door. Locked on the inside. What does that indicate to you? Now what, Mr Holmes, would you deduce from that?

Holmes That someone is trying to confuse you, Lestrade — a relatively simple task, but nonetheless ...

Lestrade (*bridling, but ignoring the slight*) You were alone — with the deceased. (*He goes to a table, picks up Moriarty's sword-stick and makes notes*) Murder weapon. Last seen in the possession of the accused ... of *you*, Holmes. Tomkins, clear the doorway, if you would!

Tomkins Come on now. Move along ... There's nothing more to see ...

The crowd disperses

Tomkins closes the door

Lestrade (*moving to the easel and looking at the portrait*) I gather you have known the young lady in question for some considerable time.

Holmes *Which young lady?*

Lestrade The portrait painter.

Holmes Yes, yes, I knew *her*.

Lestrade (*looking at the picture*) The great detective! We'll have you in our rogues' gallery up the Yard, Holmes. You shall hang there ... (*he snaps his notebook shut*) as *well* as in Wandsworth Prison!

Holmes I'm glad to see you have developed a sense of humour, Lestrade.

Lestrade Are you, Holmes?

Holmes I've always believed your work had more of a future in the music halls.

Lestrade I've always been too generous with you, Holmes. Given you the benefit of the doubt. Allowed you to take the credit for far too many of the cases *I* really solved.

Holmes (*innocently*) Just as you are solving this one. I'm sure you haven't failed to notice the bloodstains ...

Lestrade (*smugly*) There *weren't* any bloodstains.

Holmes Exactly! I'm sure that's what you haven't failed to notice.

Lestrade Not trying to be clever, are you, Holmes?

Holmes I don't *have* to try, Lestrade — *you* do! At the moment, this whole situation resembles nothing so much as an Italian comic opera.

Lestrade (*with a snort of triumph*) Italian opera, eh? You give yourself away nicely, Holmes.

Holmes Do I?

Lestrade (*opening his notebook and reading*) "An Italian opera singer who lives nearby called at the local station. She heard you quarrelling with the young lady who occupied this studio. She heard threats."

Holmes (*ironically*) No doubt she recognized my voice! It's so well known at La Scala, Milan.

Lestrade Very droll, Holmes. She distinctly heard the young lady pleading with you. "Please don't!" She cried pitifully. "Please don't kill me, Mr Holmes!"

Holmes "Mr Holmes?" That seems a remarkably formal address to use to a vengeful lover.

Lestrade Oh, so you were her *lover*! You *admit* it!

Holmes I admit nothing of the sort. (*Pause*) Did The Opera House, Wakefield and *Lucia di Lammermoor* come up in this conversation, by any chance?

Lestrade (*totally bewildered*) *What*?

Holmes (*thoughtfully*) Oh, nothing ... It's just that an old friend of mine was married to an Italian opera singer once.

Lestrade (*quietly seething*) Holmes! I can make this rough for you. I can have you in solitary for resisting arrest. I can have you on "C" diet till the day of your trial. On the other hand, if you care to co-operate ...

Holmes (*still thinking of other things*) Yes ...?

Lestrade There's a way of getting a half-bottle of brown ale a day issued in the condemned cell, if you get my meaning. Seein' as it's a gentleman to be topped.

Holmes (*with gentle sarcasm*) Well, *thank* you, Lestrade! Of course, that puts an entirely different complexion on the whole matter!

Lestrade Holmes, are you prepared to make a statement? Not that there's not enough evidence in this room alone. But there's always something tidy about a signed confession.

Holmes (*carefully knocking out his pipe, seeming to have come to a decision*) Lestrade.

Lestrade *Mister* Lestrade, Holmes.

Holmes (*putting the pipe back in his pocket*) Very well. Lestrade, do you want to know the truth about this affair?

Lestrade (*opening his notebook and starting to write*) "I make this statement voluntarily, having been warned ——"

Holmes I would prefer to confess to you alone, Inspector. Less embarrassing.

Lestrade That's better, Holmes — a little co-operation. Very well. Wait downstairs, Tomkins, Bottomley.

The two Policemen exit. Their boots are heard going downstairs

Holmes is left alone with Lestrade

(*Writing again*) "— that anything I say will be taken down and used in evidence against me." Now your statement.

Holmes My statement is this: If I, Sherlock Holmes, committed a crime ... can you possibly conceive that it would be such a bungled affair as could be solved even by the questionable talents of a *Lestrade*?

Lestrade grimly, carefully, puts away his notebook

Have you not the wit to see, man? The very fact that this affair incriminates me so neatly, in *itself* proves my entire innocence!

Lestrade brings a pair of handcuffs out of his pocket

Give me twenty-four hours' freedom. That's all I ask — and three full pipes before my fire in Baker Street ...

Lestrade moves to Holmes in order to clip the other handcuff on Holmes's wrist. He steps up on to the model's throne beside him

Lestrade I'll give you the dock in the Old Bailey, Holmes. And six foot of unmarked earth by the wall in Wandsworth. I'm not an overly patient man with murderers! (*He grabs Holmes's wrist*) Come on, man. I'm not here to listen to your flights of fancy. Get the darbies on!

Holmes now exercises his considerable knowledge of the Japanese art of Baritsu. He grabs Lestrade's wrists, gives two quick twists, there is a mechanical click and, before Lestrade realizes exactly what's happening, he is neatly handcuffed by both wrists to the model's throne. Holmes slips free and stands up

Holmes (*smiling*) I have studied with the great Houdini, Lestrade. And written a small monograph on the use of keys, chains and handcuffs——
Lestrade (*outraged, humiliated, blustering*) I must warn you, Holmes, interfering with an officer in the execution of his duty is a criminal offence, punishable by law!

Holmes slowly stuffs Lestrade's long scarf into his mouth as he speaks

Holmes (*languidly*) That's hardly a matter of great concern to a con-demned murderer, Lestrade. After all, I'm a *desperate* man!

Lestrade tries to talk, but can make only heavily muffled complaints. Holmes carefully pours the remains of the hot toddy into a corked chemical phial he produces from his pocket. He then feels in Lestrade's top pocket, brings out the key of the handcuffs, goes to the stove, opens it and drops the key in

When I have solved this little crime for you, you are most welcome to claim the entire credit for having done so — while handcuffed to the murder chair. Now *that*, my dear Lestrade, is quite an achievement!

He moves to the door, dons Lestrade's hat and coat, and places his own deerstalker and ulster around the shoulders of the incoherently protesting Lestrade. He opens the door and calls out in Lestrade's voice (NB either pre-record Lestrade speaking the following lines for Holmes to lip-synch, or have Holmes achieve a near-perfect imitation of Lestrade's voice)

Bottomley! Watch him like a hawk!

There is the clump of heavy footsteps, and Bottomley instantly reappears

Holmes points dramatically at the back of the bound, gagged and struggling Lestrade

He's dangerous! He's killed once — he'll kill again! I'll be back with the maximum security squad. Carry on, Bottomley!
Bottomley Yes, sir!

Bottomley snaps to a smart salute as Holmes departs even more smartly

Lestrade, in the deerstalker and ulster, continues to struggle as Bottomley saunters up behind him

Bottomley (*with heavy sarcasm*) So much for the Great Detective, eh? (*He shakes his head*) What I still don't understand, Mr Holmes, is how you could let yourself get caught by a total idiot like Lestrade!

SCENE 2

Outside 221B Baker Street

Mrs Hudson, Wiggins, Mossop and a couple of other Irregulars are grouped around a large open newspaper held by Wiggins, reading the front page story in disbelief. They sing in breathless horror

Song 11: Sherlock Holmes (Reprise)

Irregulars Sherlock 'Olmes
Mrs Hudson It can't be true —

Irregulars	Sherlock 'Olmes!
Mossop	Wot did 'e do?
Irregulars	Sherlock 'Olmes 'As gone an' done a rather nasty crime!
Mrs Hudson	I fear the great detective's In for a rather nasty time!
Wiggins	Accordin' to reports There was a lotta blood an' gore —
Mrs Hudson	An' poor Miss Bella Spellgrove Ain't so bella anymore!
Irregulars	An' why ain't Bella bella anymore?
Mossop	Sherlock 'Olmes — Apparently — 'As gone an' done 'er in!
Mrs Hudson	An' murder 'ere in England Is regarded as a sin!
Wiggins	'Is fate is in the 'ands Of London's evil legal gnomes!
Irregulars	It don't look good For Sherlock 'Olmes!
Mrs Hudson	'Cos London women'll Call 'im criminal —
All	Sherlock 'Olmes!

The musical commotion builds as two more Irregulars — the newsboys from Victoria Station — burst upon the scene carrying the latest editions, beside themselves with excitement

Newsboys Extra! Extra! Darin' escape of Sherlock 'Olmes! Famous detective on the run from the police! Sensation! Extra! Read all about it!

All	Sherlock 'Olmes — As usual — 'As got us all in awe — 'E's doin' what 'e's best at — Runnin' rings around the law!
Mrs Hudson	(*looking at the newspapers in mingled horror and glee*) 'E's got away with murder!

	An' 'e's got away as well!
	An' down in Scotland Yard,
	No doubt,
	They're raisin' merry 'ell!
Irregulars	An' 'oo's the reason
	For the nasty smell?
	Sherlock 'Olmes —
	I 'ate to say —
Mrs Hudson	Is really on the run!
	I can't believe
	The evil deed
	They're telling us 'e's done!
All	So pray for Bella Spellgrove
	At Saint Paul's and other domes —
	An' curse the name of
	Sherlock Holmes!
Various	It's quite a chiller!
	A fair ole thriller!
	Society's pillar —
	A lady killer!
	The great detective —
	Sherlock 'Olmes!
Irregulars	Sherlock 'Olmes —
Mrs Hudson	'E's met 'is match!
Irregulars	Sherlock 'Olmes —
Mrs Hudson	(*smugly*) But can they catch
All	Sherlock 'Olmes?!

The Lights cross-fade to:

SCENE 3

Holmes's rooms in Baker Street

Watson is staring miserably out of the window. It is raining heavily. The doorbell rings below. Shaking his head grimly, he turns back into the room and picks up an open copy of The Times *from the sofa, shaking his head in disbelief*

Watson Holmes ... a *murderer*? The world's greatest detective — the world's most brutal *criminal*? Butchering a beauty like Bella Spellgrove with a *sword-stick*? *Unthinkable*! ... *Why*? ... What possible *motivation* could he have?

There is a tap at the door

Come!

Mrs Hudson enters

Mrs Hudson (*with some disdain*) Some man to see you, doctor.
Watson I can't see anyone now, Mrs Hudson.
Mrs Hudson Says it's very important! Wouldn't take no for an answer.

Watson frowns as a doddery old Chelsea Pensioner hobbles in, wearing his scarlet uniform and walking with a stick. The Pensioner, who has a large white moustache and side whiskers, sinks, with a terrible wheezing cough, into a chair

Mrs Hudson exits

Watson (*less than pleased*) Yes, my man?
Chelsea Pensioner It's me tubes, guv'nor. They're all bunged up. That 'orrible woman at yer insultin' rooms said you was 'ere!
Watson (*unamused*) That was my wife.
Chelsea Pensioner (*with subdued laughter*) Oh. Sorry, sir.
Watson (*testily*) And I am here in a private and *not* a professional capacity! However, since you're wearing campaign medals from the Indian Mutiny, I cannot deny an old comrade ... (*He takes a spatula from his medical bag on the desk*) Open your mouth and say "ah".
Chelsea Pensioner Aaah ... (*his voice changes to that of Holmes*) ... you not glad to see me, old comrade? (*He removes his hat and whiskers and hurries over to his chemistry table*)

Watson steps back in shock, then looks sadly across at Holmes as the latter takes out the glass phial containing the hot toddy specimen. He starts to analyse it, pouring it into two different test tubes

Watson Ah, Holmes ... I was indeed glad to see you when you returned from the jaws of death at the Reichenbach Falls. But now ... I almost wish ... (*He shakes his head and turns away*)

Holmes (*gently*) That I had not survived that particular encounter? I see. The worst part of joining the murdering classes would be the loss of your friendship, doctor.

Watson (*turning on him angrily*) That poor girl, Holmes. That beautiful, young, innocent person!

Holmes Beautiful, no question. Young, beyond a shadow of a doubt. But innocent, Watson, I think not!

Watson I can hardly believe this has happened, Holmes. (*He reluctantly takes the service revolver from the pipe-rack, torn between his horror of the situation and his loyalty to Holmes*) God knows, you have no loyaller friend than I, but I can't just stand by while this horror hangs over us. It is my duty by law ... to summon the police.

Holmes doesn't even look up

Holmes "The law", Watson, as Mr Bumble so shrewdly observed many years ago, and as Inspector Lestrade reminds us on a daily basis, "is a ass". Our job, yours and mine, is to *solve* crimes, not compound them. Now be a good fellow, I beg you, and withdraw your artillery and allow me to analyse this liquid.

Watson, more by force of habit than conviction, does so, but his anger is growing

Watson (*fearfully*) You're not *listening* to me, Holmes! Your preoccupation suggests guilt!

Holmes (*snapping back*) My preoccupation suggests I wish to analyse Miss Bella Spellgrove's latest patent brand of hot toddy, which I suspect may contain one more ingredient than an unwitting consumer might anticipate. Here, Watson, *you* analyse it *for* me! If I'm right, the resultant liquid will turn bright blue!

Now intrigued, Watson puts down the revolver and takes over the experiment as Holmes steps away from the table of chemicals

Watson Our Miss Spellgrove seems to have somewhat ruffled your reasoning, Holmes.

Holmes (*snapping again*) Nonsense! Not at all! Not the least bit!

Watson Ah! So you admit it!

Holmes It was an extraordinary sensation, Watson — something between the rarefied air of a very great height and the onset of a feverish bout of influenza. As someone who has been four times trapped into wedlock, you must have experienced this malady.

Watson (*gloomily*) Almost daily. You were in love, Holmes!

Holmes (*defensively*) Nonsense, man! Though I will admit I did experience considerable pleasure in her company, enhanced by a temporary loss of reason.

Watson (*nodding sagely*) The classic symptoms.

Holmes She intrigues me, Watson. She plays games.

Watson (*perking up*) What, you mean like cricket? Jolly nice idea — a lady wicket-keeper.

Holmes No, no, no, Watson. Games of the *mind*!

Watson (*disappointed*) Oh, *them*!

Music begins under the following: "No Reason". Watson becomes increasingly absorbed with his analysis. Holmes paces the floor, agitated, upset at the dawning realization that Watson may well be right

Holmes (*muttering*) Maybe it's *myself* I should be analysing.

Song 12: No Reason

> A woman is a mystery
> That we know cannot be solved —
> And that's why I resolved
> The resolution I resolved.
> A woman is a case
> In which one should not get ...
> Involved —
> For if one does,
> One's resolution
> Tends to get dissolved.

(*Speaking*) Where was I? Oh, yes. You see what I mean, Watson? Confusion!

A man thinks much more clearly
On his own —
I need to solve my mysteries alone ...
Alone ... alone ... alone ...

There is no reason to speak of love,
If there is no love
To speak of.

There is no reason
To talk of spring —
After all, spring is just another season.

There is no reason
To think of her —
Who's to say I've got to?
But every time
I think of her,
I see no reason not to.

There is no reason
To change my life —
To let her re-arrange my life —
But wiser men than I have learned
That, where a woman is concerned,
There is no reason ...

No reason ... No reason ... No reason ...

The music continues as Watson nears the conclusion of the experiment

Watson You're right, Holmes. Women are *not* reasonable! No-one
knows that better than I! My own wife — er, Mary, I think her name is
— just threw me out of her house for no better reason than that I am —
or was — your friend. That's why I'm here.

Holmes And I thought you had been restlessly pacing the floor, worried
sick about my welfare and my fate, Watson.

Watson (*embarrassed*) Well, no. I — er — had nowhere else to go, actually ...

Holmes I have no particular knowledge of the present whereabouts of Miss Spellgrove, Watson — but I have reason to think that she is very much alive!

Watson But you were found in a *locked room* with the body of this unfortunate young lady!

Holmes With the body of *an* unfortunate young lady, Watson — clothed, I grant you, in Miss Spellgrove's continental fashion, with her hair similarly dressed, and bearing a strong family resemblance! But *not* the young lady who gave me that incipient influenza, Watson. Not at all *that* young lady!

Watson Holmes, is this true?

Holmes (*moving urgently to Watson*) You know the fellows at Bart's, Watson. You dine and sup with the police doctors. See the dead girl, I beg you. Note her face carefully! And then bring me news of the cause of her death.

Watson The cause of her death? You mean you don't *know*?

Holmes Do you want them to brand me guilty before I'm proven innocent? Only the French do that! You're not a Frenchman, are you?

Watson (*incensed*) Good God, no! Of *course* not! Damned frogs! (*His eyes widen as he pours the final result of the experiment into a glass container. He holds it up to the light. The liquid is bright blue*) My God, Holmes! It's blue! That means your famous hot toddy was laced with hycoscyamine, mixed with an opiate derivative of atropine. No taste, no smell ——

Holmes — and no trace in the body to prove I was drugged. Brilliant!

There is a knock on the door. Holmes hurriedly grabs his Chelsea Pensioner's jacket and goes back to his chair and starts wheezing

Mrs Hudson enters

Mrs Hudson It's Inspector Lestrade, doctor. He says he won't be kept waiting.

Watson Just one moment, Mrs Hudson.

She exits

Holmes (*hissing to Watson*) Lestrade will want to know if I've been here!

Lestrade bursts into the room, accompanied by PCs Bottomley and Tomkins

Lestrade pushes his way past Mrs Hudson. He is dressed in Holmes's deerstalker and ulster, which he flings to the floor in a rage as Holmes rams his Pensioner hat on his head at the last second, resuming the character of the Chelsea Pensioner. He stares up at Lestrade

Lestrade (*glaring at Watson*) I want to know if he's been here!
Watson Lestrade, I have a patient ...

Lestrade starts to look around the room, opening doors and a tall cupboard. Holmes wheezes and buries his face in a large spotted handkerchief

Holmes It's me tubes, doctor. They're all bunged up. Maybe I should take some o' this blue stuff ... (*He reaches for the experiment liquid and repeats his terrible wheezing cough*)
Watson (*hastily scribbling out a prescription*) No, no, no! Here, my man. Get this made up at the chemist. We'll see if (*pointedly*) I can help you ...
Lestrade Help the gentleman out, Bottomley. (*He opens the door*)

Holmes takes the prescription and hobbles towards the exit

Holmes Thank you, mate. You know, you bobbies are gettin' younger every day!

Holmes exits, assisted by Bottomley, who also exits

Watson A fine soldier, Lestrade. With memories of the mutiny.
Lestrade Never mind *him*. What about Holmes? I've got half of London out looking for him. That devil's vanished into thin air! He hasn't called? Left a message in any way? Got in touch?

Pause

Watson (*carefully and truthfully*) I have seen no-one — but that patient.
Lestrade No, of course he hasn't! Holmes is far too clever to come here of all places. (*Through gritted teeth*) I'll get him! It's only a matter of

time! (*He confides in Watson*) Locked in my own darbies! They had to send for a blacksmith!

Watson (*casually*) Lestrade, I was wondering ——

Lestrade (*in disgust*) A blacksmith! To release a Scotland Yard inspector from his own handcuffs! Humiliating stuff, Watson. Humiliating!

Watson (*amused*) Humiliating stuff indeed, Lestrade! Tell me, who's the medical man dealing with this enquiry?

Lestrade Why?

Watson (*holding up the blue liquid*) I may be able to be of some assistance.

Lestrade Doctor Martingdale is the police medico. (*He moves to the door*)

Watson "Boffy" Martingdale? He and I played in the scrum at Bart's. Mrs Hudson, my hat and coat. Good old Boffy! Thank you, Lestrade.

Lestrade (*in deep frustration*) Humiliating!

He follows Watson from the room as Mrs Hudson enters. She treats him to a seductive smile as he exits

Mrs Hudson (*to herself*) Now there's a passionate man!

She muses as she watches him leave. The musical vamp begins

Song 13: A Lousy Life (Reprise)

Mrs Hudson   Can you imagine
                         Marryin' a man
                         'Oo's at Scotland Yard ? —
                         That everyone accounts to?

                         Can you imagine
                         'Avin' an 'usband-cum-bodyguard?
                         Well, that's what it amounts to!

                         Someone 'oo's proven,
                         True, tried an' tested!
                         Pride o' the police force —
                         As 'e 'as attested!
                         Wonder if 'e's interested?
                         With my luck, I'd be arrested!

Could 'appen ter me!
Only ter me!
You got to agree!
I'll admit it — I'm ...
(*In a confidential whisper*) Fifty-three!
Time keeps flyin' —
I keep tryin' —
Eyein' any man 'oo could use a wife!

Mine 'as been a dismal,
Totally abysmal,
Close to cataclysmal,
Gettin' rheumatismal,
Truly — lousy — life!

The Lights cross-fade to:

SCENE 4

Somewhere in London

Holmes appears, dressed in his usual clothes, and seemingly in the very best of high spirits. He positively glows with a newly returned confidence. There is appropriately up-tempo music under the following

Holmes (*with relish*) All right, Miss Bella. You want to play games?
   We'll play games! Maybe more than you bargained for!

Song 14: My Incomparable Best

At last! At last! The stage is set
For an intellectual battle
That the world will not forget.
My opponent — Moriarty, the epitome of evil —
Combines the ways of Satan
With the habits of a weevil.

I will need to summon
All the many skills of my profession —

To be sharp as Moriarty's,
To be sharper than a knife.
In these very strange conditions,
I've a very strange confession —
I have never felt so happy in my life!

For these are circumstances
Under which I thrive.
A man so close to death
Becomes aware that he's alive.
And Sherlock Holmes is very much alive!

There's a panther-like spring in my walk.
There is infinite charm in my voice when I talk,
And I gaze at the world
With the all-seeing eye
Of a lonely and high-flying hawk.

I'm discreetly but stylishly dressed —
When I look at myself, I confess I'm impressed!
And in fact I would say
That you see me today
When I'm at my incomparable best!

I have manners befitting a prince.
I have flair without flourish,
And charm without chintz.
I adjusted my necktie at teatime today —
I have not seen such elegance since.

It's a little bit sad for the rest.
When they see me they must be extremely depressed.
I am taste at its peak —
The quintessence of chic —
When I'm at my incomparable best!

The music swells as Holmes rubs his hands grimly and looks around him in anticipation

All right, Miss Moriarty —
It is time to start the party —
The final confrontation between you and me!
And I hope, Miss Moriarty,
That you're feeling hale and hearty,
Because that's the very least you'll need to be —
If you intend,
My evil friend,
To see the end of me!

You've picked a rather silly time
To put me to the test —
A time, alas, when I'm
At my incomparable best!

There's a trace of a smile on my face —
And I hold the whole world
In my worldly embrace —
As I travel through life
With a rare combination
Of modesty, sweetness and grace.

I have never been put to the test,
But I know there is nobody so self-possessed,
So incredibly right,
As myself on a night
When I'm at my incomparable best!

Personality, sparkle and poise,
With a dash of panache and the minimum noise,
Are the wonderful weapons that win me the day
In the war everybody enjoys.

I would humbly presume to suggest
What discerning observers have already guessed —
That the culture of man
Becomes all that it can
When I'm at my incomparable best!

When I'm at my very
Bright and merry
Legendary
Best!

SCENE 5

The morgue at Bart's

Watson's old friend, Dr "Boffy" Martingdale, is conducting a post-mortem with the help of a white-coated Assistant, who is taking notes

Watson enters dripping with rain, and shakes his umbrella

Martingdale The presence of a massive subdural haematoma is consistent with the deceased having received a heavy blow with a blunt instrument in the occipital region of the skull ...

Watson (*looking around nostalgically*) Ah, the morgue! It's like being back home ... *Boffy*! My dear old Boffy!

Martingdale (*looking up in surprise*) Good God! "Embrocation" Watson! That's what we used to call you! When the probationer nurses got tired, you volunteered to massage their legs with Ellerman's Athletic Rub ... Won't shake hands, Watson — bit messy!

Watson (*wistfully*) Halcyon days, Boffy — halcyon days! But I regret to say I'm now a happily married man. (*He thinks about it*) Least, I *think* I am! (*He looks around*) The dear old morgue! Such happy memories!

Martingdale Scene of some of our best parties! One place you could take a nurse without Staff Sister running after you ... (*To the Assistant*) Thank you, Crippen.

Watson removes and shakes his soaking wet topcoat and bowler hat, and throws them carelessly over a shrouded cadaver. He moves the cadaver's legs to one side and perches on the end of the slab beside it, as though sitting on a friend's bed. Martingdale indicates for the Assistant to leave

The Assistant exits

Watson And the weather isn't any better now than it was then! You know, Boffy, I've always attributed my rheumatism to that romp in the rain with Nurse Jenkins in June of sixty-six!

Martingdale And my gout and arthritis to drinking port with Nurse Merriweather on that marble slab over there in September of sixty-seven!

Watson They say there are three things in England that will never improve: the food, the weather and the fast bowling!

Martingdale (*taking his coat*) Well, at least the other two don't make you wet!

Watson (*patting a slab affectionately*) No doubt about it, Boffy — they were golden days!

Martingdale (*gleefully*) Well, all is not lost, old boy! It just so happens ... (*he opens a cadaver drawer and produces a bottle of port and two glasses*) *Voilà*, as the frogs say. Taylor's seventy-five!

Watson (*beaming*) You haven't got Nurse Merriweather in there too, by any chance, have you?

Martingdale Don't see why not — she's old enough!

They both roar with noisy juvenile laughter as Martingdale pours two very large killer drinks. They raise their glasses

My dear old Watson — to good times gone by!

Watson (*clinking glasses*) Any port in a storm, as you used to say!

Martingdale Down in one, remember.

After further rowdy roars of laughter, they down their giant drinks in a single prolonged gulp as the music begins jauntily

Song 15: Halcyon Days

Watson	They were the best of times —
Martingdale	They were the worst of times —
Watson	And the most blessed of times —
Martingdale	And the most cursed of times!
Watson	We'd get depressed at times —
Martingdale	And overjoyed at times —
Watson	Riding the crest at times —
Martingdale	Facing the void at times!
Both	Those were halcyon days!
	Let's sing the praise

                    Of our halcyon days!
                    Here's to pal-seein' days!
                    Oh, to go back again
                    And take another crack again
                    At those heavenly halcyon days!

Martingdale refills their glasses

Martingdale	Life was serene at times —
Watson	And quite obscene at times!
Martingdale	True, we would shirk at times —
Watson	P'raps even work at times!
Martingdale	We'd chat up girls at times —
Watson	Say we were earls at times —
Martingdale	If they got fed at times —
Watson	Popped 'em in bed at times!
Both	Good old halcyon days!
	How my mind strays
	To those halcyon days!
	Gorgeous gal-seein' days!
Martingdale	Oh, to be young again! —
Watson	And have Nurse Brown relieve the pain! —
	Like she did in those halcyon days!

They roar with laughter, clink glasses and down their drinks. Once more
Martingdale refills the glasses

Martingdale	We were insane at times —
Watson	Runaway train at times —
Martingdale	But how we used those times!
Watson	Though we abused those times!
Martingdale	Though they are gone, at times —
Watson	Memory lives on, at times —
Martingdale	Though we get sad at times —
Both	Thank God we had those times!
	Dear old halcyon days!
	They were amazing,
	Our halcyon days!

	Priceless pal-seein' days!
Martingdale	If there's another life —
Watson	Can I have mine without the wife?

There is a terrifying thunderclap

(*Speaking; timidly*) Sorry, Mary — only joking!

More roars of laughter. Down go the drinks. One last refill

Both	God-sent halcyon days!
	Life was ablaze
	In our halcyon days!
	Treasure pal-seein' days!
Martingdale	Wastin' 'em's worse than theft!
Watson	We may not have that many left! —
	Like we did in those halcyon days!

They raise their glasses one final time

Both	Here's to those
Martingdale	Once-only,
Watson	Un-lonely,
Martingdale	Eye-poppin',
Watson	Heart-stoppin',
Martingdale	Fun-fateful,
Watson	Ungrateful,
Martingdale	Life-driven,
Watson	God-given,
Martingdale	Best,
Watson	Worst,
Martingdale	Blessed,
Watson	Cursed,
Both	Pal-seein',
	Gal-seein',
	Bart's hospital-seein',
	Glorious halcyon
	Days!

They drain their drinks and collapse in each other's arms. Decidedly the worse for wear, Watson pulls himself together and gives his old chum Boffy a pat on the back

Watson I don't know whether it's you or the morgue, Boffy, but I'm feeling decidedly depressed — and about a hundred and fifty years old!

Martingdale (*cheerily*) But now, you haven't come back here just to talk about old times, Watson.

Watson (*back to business*) No. You've — er — seen the body, I take it?

Martingdale "The Studio Stabbing Case"? I *have* met the lady, yes.

Watson She *was* stabbed, of course.

Martingdale Oh, yes. No doubt about that. Entry point under the left pectoral. Only thing that worries me is ...

Watson What?

Martingdale I'm not absolutely sure *that* was the cause of death!

Watson What are you saying, Boffy?

Martingdale The girl had advanced diptheria, the sort of thing you get from drinking the water in some filthy continental resort. It's my belief *that's* what did for her!

Watson You mean she was dead ... *before* the stab wound?

Martingdale It's a possibility. I know it seems extraordinary ——

Watson There are deep waters here, as my friend would say. Very deep waters, Boffy. Could I have a look at her?

Martingdale Of course. I'd be glad of your opinion.

Martingdale leads a reluctant Watson over and shows him the body. Music for "Her Face" begins under as Watson braces himself and looks. Then he turns away, frowning with surprise. He walks downstage as Martingdale and the morgue fade into black behind him

Watson (*deeply puzzled*) It's *not* her! ... And if it's not her, who *is* it? ... And if it's not her, *where* is she?

He picks up his umbrella and walks slowly away, rapt in thought

Music: "Without Him, There Can Be No Me" begins as the Lights slowly cross-fade to:

SCENE 6

The River Thames Embankment/A street lamp in a dark street

Bella wanders slowly along the riverside, deep in thought

Song 16: Without Him, There Can Be No Me (Reprise)

Bella

I am somewhere
I have never been before —
Seeing things
That I have never seen before.
Thinking different thoughts —
Singing different songs —
And wond'ring
Where my heart belongs.

Without fire, there can be no flame!
Without players, there can be no game!
Without Shakespeare, there'd be no "To be or not to be"!
Without him, there can be no me!

Without day, there can be no night —
Without wrong, there can be no right —
Without evil, there can be no good of great degree —
Without him, there can be no me!

Without light, no dark —
Without Noah, no ark —
Without him, no spark
To relieve my gloom!
Without hope, no chance —
Without Paris, no France —
Without him, no romance
In life, I assume!

Without love, there can be no hate!
Good and ill both decide our fate!
Without him, no mystery
To which I am the key!

       Without him, no moments
       Only he can guarantee!
       So all in all, as far as I can see,
       Without him, there can be no me! (*She continues to pace
       up and down the Embankment*)

Mrs Moriarty, distraught and out of breath, appears out of the night and hurries to join her

Mrs Moriarty I look for you everywhere! 'Ee escape! Sherlock 'Olmes *escape*!

Bella cannot conceal her pleasure

Bella (*laughing; thrilled*) I don't *believe* it! The man's a *genius*! (*To her mother*) Father always said he was a foeman worthy of his steel!

Mrs Moriarty (*inconsolable*) I give the body of my poor child Maria to avenge your father's death — and the murderer escapes us! This is *funny*?

Bella (*her attitude suddenly hardening*) He's a criminal hunted like a dog, Mama! If he so much as sets foot in the street, the police will get him! Doesn't *that* satisfy you?

Mrs Moriarty When I stand in front of their prison gates and see them put up the notice "The Murderer Holmes — hanged this morning!" — *that* will satisfy me! Forget the English police! You should have killed him when you had the chance!

Bella When *we* had the chance, Mama — when *we* had the chance! But you're right! It seems we must finish this ourselves.

Mrs Moriarty London is big. Where do we look?

Bella (*musing*) For a criminal on the run? Only one place is safe — among other criminals! They have a famous meeting-place, Mama — an old pub on the Isle of Dogs. *That's* where we'll find news of Mr Sherlock Holmes! (*She smiles in sly satisfaction as her plan forms*) We shall use good to find evil. I know exactly how we'll do it!

Mrs Moriarty (*grimly*) I'll do *anything* that will 'elp to bury our enemy! And *this* time I don't let you out of my sight till it's *done*!

She marches purposefully away, followed by Bella

Music: "London Is London" begins as the Lights cross-fade to:

The Apples 'n' Pears *pub on the Isle of Dogs*

Outside the popular public house, featuring a staircase descending from the upper level to the lower. A seedy East End hangout for an unsavoury assortment of thieves and villains

The place is crowded with rowdy beer- and-gin-swilling drinkers. Mingling among them, ever on the lookout, are the Irregulars. A group of local Down-and-outs regard them with extreme hostility. Wiggins and Co. look around with amusement at the assembled company

Wiggins They're a charmin' lookin' bunch, I must say! Well, that's London fer yer!

Song 17: London Is London (Reprise)

Irregulars   London is London —
                    A meltin'-pot o' thieves an' villains!
                    Millin' round London —
                    All swillin' gin an' stealin' millions!
                    London is sleazy —
                    S'easy ter see!
                    Too free an' easy —
                    Slimy, grimy —
                    Oh, gorblimey!

The music continues under as into this unlikely environment marches a small but noisy Salvation Army band, with a Major conducting

The locals whistle and hoot derisively as the band comes to a halt. Bringing up the rear, a picture of piety, dressed in Salvation Army uniforms and pushing a small cart labelled "The Lord Abides in London — Free Coffee for All" are Bella and Mrs Moriarty. With her Salvation Army bonnet, pince-nez glasses, a red wig and a fruity cockney accent, Bella is barely recognizable. She and Mrs Moriarty take a centre position in the group, and on a cue from the Major, start to sing

Song 18: The Lord Abides in London

Salvation Army The Lord abides in London,
For London's pride is pure.
His faith resides in London —
Supreme ... secure.

Pickpockets ply their trade

Jesus's love
Is everywhere —
From Baker Street
To Soho Square.

The music of "London Is London" creeps back in under the hymn in unobtrusive counterpoint, while the Irregulars cheekily interject the words of their own "hymn" into a counter-melody

Irregulars London	**Salvation Army** The Lord provides
Is London —	In London —
Is anyone in	Of that you may
Doubt about it?	Be sure.
London	Goodwill presides
Is London —	In London —
Forgive me if I	Which will
Shout about it.	Endure.

The Lord's up in Heaven —
The Pope's down in Rome —
But the Lord abides in London —
All   'Cos London
Is London
Is England
Is home!

The crowd falls silent as the two songs end

Lestrade enters, to a detectable raspberry from the Salvation Army tuba, followed by PCs Bottomley and Tomkins

Lestrade supervises the PCs as they pin up a "Wanted" notice at the entrance to the Apples 'n' Pears. *Lestrade glares accusingly at everyone around him, then reads the notice aloud*

   As he speaks, a grubby, unshaven Costermonger enters, pushing a fruit barrow, which he parks. He listens to Lestrade

Lestrade (*pompously*) Evenin', all! (*He reads*) "A reward ... of one hundred guineas ... will be paid ... for information ... leading to the arrest of the escaped murderer, Sherlock Holmes ... in *any* condition!"
Costermonger (*calling out*) What's "any condition" mean, guv'nor? Drunk or sober?

Roars of laughter greet the question

Lestrade (*humourlessly*) It means dead or alive, my man — and this is no laughin' matter.
Costermonger I promise you, guv'nor, when people get drunk round 'ere, you can't *tell* whether they're dead or alive—an' that's no laughin' matter, neither!
Lestrade (*repeating dramatically*) One hundred guineas! Constable!

There is more raucous laughter

   Lestrade ignores the ribaldry and exits with his minions

Bella starts to dispense mugs of coffee to a quickly formed, murderous-looking queue of criminally disposed Down-and-outs

1st Down-and-out You're good to us bad 'uns, miss.
Bella Not really! When it comes to a free cuppa coffee, mate, we don't mind 'ow big a sinner yer are!
Major In fact, the bigger the sinner, the hotter and sweeter the coffee!
2nd Down-and-out Better give me four lumps then, miss. I done the Black'eath Massacre! (*He laughs copiously at this bloodthirsty reminiscence*)
Bella (*serving the sugar*) Four lumps it is! There's one other sinner I'd like to see down 'ere! 'E'd be sure of an 'ot drink an' shelter for the night, an' no mistake!

1st Down-and-out 'Oo's that then, miss?
Bella Sherlock 'Olmes, the wanted murderer.
1st Down-and-out You'd give *'im* shelter?
2nd Down-and-out I mus' say, I'm shocked!
1st Down-and-out Or are you just after them 'undred guineas?
Bella Just let 'im know 'e's got a friend 'ere. You know where 'e's been 'iding?
2nd Down-and-out (*shaking his head*) Somewhere out there in the smoke.

The Costermonger sees the coffee trolley and approaches Bella, munching an apple from his barrow

Costermonger (*amiably*) Art'noon. Black wi' no sugar for me, please, miss.
Bella This coffee's for sinners only!
Costermonger Well, in that case feel free ter gimme the 'ole bleedin' coffee pot!

The Down-and-outs roar with laughter. Bella smiles and hands the Costermonger a mug of coffee

Bella Yeah, you look like you might deserve it!
Costermonger Thank you, miss. You're a good Barnaby o' bad character.
Bella (*not understanding*) Barnaby?
Street Girl Barnaby Rudge — judge. Cockney rhymin' slang! *You* know!

The Costermonger tips his hat and points at the Apples 'n' Pears *pub. Music begins: "Down the Apples 'n' Pears". The Street Girl continues to translate for Bella, who quickly gets the hang of it*

Costermonger If this 'ere 'ostelry could ball o' chalk ...
Street Girl Talk ...
Costermonger ... my little cup o' cheer ...
Street Girl My dear ...
Costermonger ... it could bear witness to my 'orrible disgustin' nature as a Derby winner ...
Street Girl Sinner ...

Costermonger ... better'n practically any other buildin' in Newcastle
    Brown!
Street Girl London Town!

*Everybody gathers around to listen. They know a character when they
see one*

Song 19: Down the Apples 'n' Pears

Costermonger   No doubt you may be wonderin'
                     'Ow this tavern got its name —
                     It's 'cos of this 'ere staircase
                     That it made its claim to fame.

                     The landlord 'ad a daughter
                     'Oo could melt yer wiv 'er eyes —
                     An' I was bein' melted
                     When 'e took us by surprise!
                     What did I do?
                     Well, wouldn't you?

*NB The bold words of the refrain are sung by the Company, the rest by
the Costermonger*

                     'E jumped — I diddled 'n' bumped —
                     Out the Jenny Linder — **out the winder** —
                     An' 'e ran — I did a dirty ole man —
                     Down the apples 'n' pears — **down the stairs** —

                     Of the 'ouse — of the cat 'n' mouse —
                     Down the policeman's beat — **down the street** —
                     Wiv 'is trousers — wiv me round-the-'ouses —
                     Round me plates o' meat — **round 'is feet!**

                     All eyes — all the mince pies —
                     Saw me daisy roots — **saw 'is boots** —
                     An' 'is 'at — an' me tit-fer-tat —
                     In me promised land — **in 'is 'and!**

An' 'er pore ole father — 'er shavin' lather —
Gnashed 'is teeth — gnashed 'is 'Ampstead 'Eath —
Wants 'is daughter — wants 'is bottled water —
Down the lean 'n' lurch — **at the church!**

Costermonger   An' all because 'e took me unawares —
An' I fell down the apples 'n' pears!
Company   (*repeat the two-line tag*)
An' all because 'e took 'im unawares —
An' 'e fell down the apples 'n' pears!

Costermonger   An' that's the God's-truth reason
'Ow this tavern got its name —
It cured me from philanderin',
An' it got 'er off the game!
An' then one day perchance
I met a barmaid in me room —
An' wouldn't yer know the landlord
Come an' found us in full bloom!

What did I do?
Well, wouldn't you?
Company   Well, wouldn't you?

'E jumped — I diddled 'n' bumped —
Out the Jenny Linder — **out the winder** —
An' 'e ran — I did a dirty ole man —
Down the apples 'n' pears — **down the stairs** —

Of the 'ouse — of the cat 'n' mouse —
Down the policeman's beat — **down the street** —
Wiv 'is trousers — wiv me round-the-'ouses —
Round me plates o' meat — **round 'is feet!**

All eyes — all the mince pies —
Saw me daisy roots — **saw 'is boots** —
An' 'is 'at — an' me tit-fer-tat —
In me promised land — **in 'is 'and!**

> An' the pore ole landlord — the 'old-my-'and-lord —
> **Gnashed 'is teeth** — gnashed 'is 'Ampstead 'Eath —
> **Wants the barmaid** — wants the right-you-are-maid —
> Down the lean 'n' lurch — **at the church!**

Costermonger   An' all because 'e took me unawares —
An' I fell down the apples 'n' pears!

Company   (*repeat the two-line tag*)
An' all because 'e took 'im unawares —
An' 'e fell down the apples 'n' pears!

The Costermonger drags an unwilling Bella into the song and dance

Costermonger   There's one last little story
'Ow this tavern got its name —
It brings a smile of pleasure,
Though it tells a tale of shame.
The landlord's wife
Was showin' the mayor
The best room in the 'ouse —
An' there she found
A great big Irish sailor
Wiv 'er spouse!

What did 'e do?
Well, wouldn't you?

Company   Well, wouldn't you?

'E jumped — 'e diddled 'n' bumped —
Out the Jenny Linder — **out the winder** —
An' 'e ran — 'e did a dirty ole man —
Down the apples 'n' pears — **down the stairs** —

Of the 'ouse — of the cat 'n' mouse —
Down the policeman's beat — **down the street** —
Wiv 'is trousers — wiv 'is round-the-'ouses —
Round 'is plates o' meat — **round 'is feet!**

All eyes — all the mince pies —
Saw 'is daisy roots — **saw 'is boots** —

An' 'is 'at — an' 'is tit-fer-tat —
In 'is promised land — **in 'is 'and!**

An' the pore ole landlord — the 'old-my-'and-lord —
Gnashed 'is teeth — gnashed 'is 'Ampstead 'Eath —
Took the sailor — took the tinker-tailor —
Down the lean 'n' lurch — **to the church!**

An' all because
She took 'im unawares —
An' 'e fell down the apples 'n' pears!

By now Bella is right into the vernacular as well as the spirit of the song

Bella	That's the 'ope an' glory!
Company	(*in delight*) That's the story!
Bella	That's the book of Ruth!
Company	That's the truth!
Bella	'Ow this rocky cavern —
Company	'Ow this tavern —
Bella	Got its cryin' shame!
Company	Got its name!

An' all because
She took 'im unawares —
An' 'e fell down the apples 'n' pears!

An' that's why stairs
Are called apples 'n' pears!

With a signal, Wiggins gathers Mossop and the other Irregulars around him as the Down-and-outs, mightily cheered up, cluster around Bella, the Costermonger and the coffee trolley. Wiggins produces a large gold watch from his tattered pocket and consults it. As they are about to disperse, the Costermonger emerges from the group of Down-and-outs

Costermonger 'Ere you are, me old china plates — in the name o' charity an' all that's 'oly, free fruit for all!

With a rousing cheer, the Down-and-outs fall on the fruit barrow and attack its contents

PC Bottomley enters during the following

The Costermonger taps Wiggins on the shoulder

Costermonger 'Scuse me, mate, got the time? (*He draws Wiggins aside*)
Wiggins I just so 'appens I do. (*He pulls out the watch again*)

The Costermonger takes the gold watch from Wiggins and speaks in Holmes's unmistakable voice

Holmes I shall return this spectacular timepiece to Sir Jevons Jarndyce with your compliments.
Wiggins (*gaping in amazement*) Mr 'Olmes! Wot *you* done up like that fer?
Holmes One person alone on this earth, Wiggins, could cause Sherlock Holmes to be selling fruit on the Isle of Dogs.
Wiggins Moriarty.
Holmes Precisely.
Wiggins But 'e's dead! (*Pointedly*) Just like that nice Miss Bella! You butchered 'er! (*He looks at Holmes accusingly*) I can't believe you *did* that, Mr 'Olmes!
Holmes You are not *required* to believe I did that. I would prefer you to believe that I did *not*!
Wiggins (*shaking his head*) I dunno *what* to believe!
Holmes It's very simple, Wiggins. (*He points to Bottomley*) There's the law ... (*He points to the "Wanted" sign*) There's the reward ... (*He points to himself*) Turn me in and you can be on the right side of both! You can shop me — or you can help me.

Wiggins considers the situation, then crosses to Bottomley

Wiggins 'Scuse me, officer ... (*he looks meaningfully at Holmes*) I used to 'ave a watch, but someone nicked it! Can you give me the time?
Bottomley I'll give you thirty days, Wiggins — if you don't clear off!
Wiggins (*returning to Holmes*) I've thought about it ... *You* believed in *me* when it mattered, so I 'spose I'd better do the same.

Holmes (*smiling*) You display Holmesian qualities of judgement, my dear Wiggins — because not only is that nice Miss Bella *alive* and well, you have just consumed a mug of her singularly undistinguished coffee. (*He indicates Bella's coffee-cart*)

Wiggins (*stunned*) Wot, that Salvation Army bird? *That's Bella?* (*He looks from Bella to Holmes in his Costermonger garb*) Wot is this, Mr 'Olmes? A bleedin' fancy-dress ball?

Holmes (*grimly*) "Fancy *death* ball" would be a more apt phrase, Wiggins, as you will shortly discover. Now listen carefully. (*He reverts to his Costermonger voice*) This is strictly between yer old Coster mate an' yerself — you *didn't* 'ear it from that Sherlock Holmes geezer, right?

Wiggins (*nodding*) Right.

Holmes (*himself again; in an urgent whisper*) I want you and the lads to spread the word immediately — warn everybody — in every dark corner, every murderer's crib and thieves' kitchen (*he indicates the Down-and-outs still gathered around the fruit-barrow*) that Moriarty is *alive!*

Wiggins (*with a gasp*) Moriarty!?

Holmes (*nodding*) Alive and back in his rat's hole in Wapping Docks. *Everyone* must know — and most especially Miss Bella!

Wiggins (*promptly*) Right, sir!

Holmes ⎫
                  ⎬ (*together*) Consider it done.
Wiggins ⎭

Holmes turns abruptly away and is instantly totally back in the character of the Costermonger. He claps his hands as he reapproaches the fruit barrow

Costermonger All right, lads — 'ands off! I said, "free fruit for all", not put me outta bleedin' business!

The Down-and-outs move away from the barrow

Well, I must be off! Got a delivery to make at Buckin'ham Palace, don't I? Cheerio, then!

With a cheery wave and a loud chortle, he exits with the fruit barrow

Wiggins rejoins the Irregulars, audibly whispering the name Moriarty.
They repeat the name to one another, and the word spreads like wildfire
among the Down-and-outs, who point at Wiggins

The sinister theme of "He's Back!" starts under as the Down-and-outs
approach the Irregulars

1st Down-and-out (*to Wiggins*) Did I 'ear you whisper the magic name
  o' Moriarty, my lad?
Wiggins (*acting scared*) You did, mate! An' it's *true*!

The music builds into a sinister Gregorian chant as the evil musical word
about Moriarty's return spreads slowly and inexorably around the group,
until the impact of the news dominates everything

Song 20: He's Back

Irregulars } He's back! — Moriarty!
Company } He's back! — Moriarty!

                  The black-hearted architect
                  Of countless crimes —
                  The fiend who's corrupted justice
                  Countless times —
                  The leader
                  Of the world's most evil pack —
                  That venemous thing —
                  The uncrowned king
                  Of untold crime
                  Is back! Moriarty!
                  He's back — He's back! — He's back!
                  Moriarty is back!

                  The police will cease
                  To sleep in peace —
                  They'll run around
                  Like headless geese —
                  And crime
                  Will instantly increase.

The building climax of the chant is timed by the Irregulars to reach Bella's notice at this point. It does

> The one crook
> Sherlock Holmes
> Can't crack —
> He's back! Moriarty!
> He's back! Moriarty!
> He's back!
>
> Moriarty is back!

Finally Bella hears the name. She drops a mug of coffee, which crashes and breaks on the ground

Bella Did you say ... Professor Moriarty?
Wiggins That's right, miss. 'E's definitely back.

> *A police whistle sounds. The Down-and-outs scatter*
>
> *The Sergeant pushes the coffee trolley away and exits*

Bella moves downstage, where the Down-and-outs are chattering together. She now resumes her usual accent. The need for subterfuge is over

Bella I need your help.
1st Down-and-out For you, lady, anything!
Bella Have any of you heard of Wapping Docks?
1st Down-and-out (*taking her arm*) 'Eard of 'em? I was *born* there!
Bella (*urgently*) Will you take me there, please?
1st Down-and-out (*amazed*) *Take* yer there? I spent 'arf me bleedin' life tryin' ter get *away* from the place! 'Snot safe! 'Sfulla people like *me*!
Bella (*coolly*) Don't worry — I'll take care of you!
1st Down-and-out Wild 'orses couldn't get me ter ——
Bella (*holding up a coin*) A guinea?
1st Down-and-out But *that* could!

He takes the coin and her arm and they exit together as the music segués back into the sinister motif of "He's Back!"

As Bella vanishes from view, Holmes and Watson emerge from the Apples 'n' Pears, Holmes now dressed in his usual street apparel, and Watson stuffing the Costermonger's hat and jacket into a Gladstone bag. Holmes smiles as he sees Bella depart. Watson looks around in concern as they move into a darker area of Dockland

Holmes So I was right, Watson. The autopsy confirms my theory?

Watson Beyond any shadow of doubt! (*Dubiously*) You know, I can never forgive myself for mistrusting you, Holmes.

Holmes No, no, no, my dear fellow! For one nasty moment, I almost mistrusted myself! I must say it's reassuring to know that one's powers of deduction remain infallible. Her plan was brilliant. (*He starts to pace back and forth with great energy, a smile of grudging admiration on his face*)

Watson watches him closely, trying to figure it all out

(*Musing*) Simply brilliant! And brilliantly simple! Like most great puzzles, Watson — so obvious, yet so hard to see.

Watson (*in a total fog*) Absolutely, Holmes ... er — what is, old boy?

Holmes The whereabouts of Moriarty ...

Watson (*baffled*) But you just said that ——

Holmes Moriarty is dead. Yes, I did.

Watson (*relieved*) Ah! *Well* then ...

Holmes But Moriarty *lives*!

Watson (*confused again*) Oh!

Holmes *That's* what's so clever!

Watson It is, isn't it?

Holmes It's perfect! What more could one ask, Watson?

Watson (*blinking*) What more, indeed! Not a lot, I suppose. Moriarty is dead, but Moriarty lives.

Holmes There's not much escapes you, is there, old friend?

Watson Apart from the fact that I don't know what I'm talking about, no!

Holmes It's good to see you back on form, Watson.

Watson Thank you, Holmes. I didn't realize I was!

Holmes takes an envelope from his inside pocket and hands it to Watson

Holmes In the circumstances, I cannot risk entrusting the capture of Moriarty to Lestrade. This time there can be no mistake. I must do it myself. Watson, take this note immediately to Lestrade, and beg him with all urgency to do *exactly* as I ask. No improvisations. Have him bring his men to this address in Wapping in precisely one hour and twenty minutes from now and surround the building.

Watson reacts promptly to the tone of Holmes's voice and takes the envelope

Watson Certainly, old boy. I haven't seen you this perky since you solved that very tricky business of "The Man with the Twisted Lip"!
Holmes This one's even trickier, Watson. But then so am I!

Dark, sinister music begins under as they exit

The Lights cross-fade to:

SCENE 8

A deserted warehouse — Wapping Docks

The dark, threatening music of "He's Back!" introduces the deserted warehouse that is used by Professor Moriarty as his headquarters during his occasional trips to London. There is a low bridge over a canal leading out of the nearby River Thames. Elsewhere, there are racks which contain shotguns, pistols and large, draped packing-cases marked "Danger — Explosives". Rats scuttle, and the sinister sound of dripping water echoes endlessly through the dank, cavernous building

Mrs Moriarty appears with the 2nd Down-and-out, calling out her husband's name

Mrs Moriarty James?... James?... Where are you, caro?

The echoes of the words repeat, intermingling with the dripping of the water. There is no reply

The 2nd Down-and-out receives the second half of his reward from Mrs Moriarty and departs

Mrs Moriarty searches on in the gloom alone and disappears from view

A moment later, Bella appears, escorted by the 1st Down-and-out, who looks decidedly nervous alongside the cool, unruffled Bella

1st Down-and-out You quite sure you want ter be 'ere, miss?
Bella (*nodding*) *Quite* sure. Thank you, my friend. You go now. This is no place for you.
1st Down-and-out (*willingly departing*) You're right about that! That's why I left 'ere in the first place! 'Snough to give yer the creeps!

He exits

Bella (*calling*) Father?... Father ... Father, where are you? It's me, Bella ... Father ... Father ...

Moriarty's voice, weak but recognizable, calls from out of the darkness

Moriarty (*off*) Bella!...

Bella looks up excitedly. The music continues under. Bella turns at the sound of a door opening

Out of the shadows appears a hunched figure in a wheelchair. There is a rug on his knees — but the high forehead, the wispy white hair, and the dark glasses make it unmistakeably clear that Professor Moriarty has arrived on the scene

Bella starts towards him

Moriarty Bella!
Bella (*excitedly*) Father! I never thought I'd see you again!

When Moriarty speaks from the shadows, it is clearly the same voice we heard at the Reichenbach Falls

Moriarty (*with a grim chuckle*) Life is full of surprises, Bella. But I am not the man I was, alas. The Reichenbach Falls did some little damage. (*He holds up his hand for Bella to keep her distance*) Stay, my child. Let me look at you. You have become so very grown-up ...

Bella (*smiling*) I have missed you, Father.

Moriarty And I have neglected *you*, my dear. Something I regret more than I can say.

Song 21: A Million Years Ago — or Was It Yesterday?

Moriarty
> A million years ago —
> Or was it yesterday?
> I saw you
> As I see you now —
> Just the same —
> But changed somehow —
> Don't come any closer —
> But don't go away!

Bella
> A million dreams ago —
> Or was it one or two?
> I dreamed a dream
> And it was you —
> Just a dream
> But it came true!
> Don't come any closer —
> Unless you can stay!
>
> Unless you can stay!
> Unless there's a way!
> Unless you say
> It's forever —
> And never
> Go away!

Moriarty
> A million lives ago
> I know we met before —
> And yet before
> I let you go,

                                One more thing
                                I have to know —
                                Was it yesterday —
                                Or a million years ago?

Both   A million years ago?
                                Or only yesterday?
Moriarty   It was yesterday!
Bella   Only yesterday!
Both   But I've missed you so
                                That it seems like a million years ago!

There is a long moment of silence as the emotional moment between them registers strongly

Holmes appears in the shadows on the upper bridge level and looks down on them, overhearing their conversation

Bella (*suddenly sobbing*) It has been so difficult without you, Father. Poor Maria.

Moriarty (*nodding sympathetically*) I know. You have done well, my child.

Bella (*becoming angry*) Done *well*? Oh, yes ... We have done *very* well, Mama and I. We drugged him. We left him with poor dead Maria in a locked room. So *considerate* of my sister to *die* so we could set a trap for Mr Holmes ... *Lucky*, weren't we? We tied a rope so neatly round his neck! Isn't that what you wanted?

Moriarty Exactly what I wanted.

Bella But it was all for nothing, wasn't it? It was just a game — it's all a game, for both of you! He never killed you. He *couldn't* kill you! And *you* can't kill him! He's alive! ... Somewhere he's alive! Just like you! But too clever for you. He's too clever for you, Father ...

During the following, Watson stealthily enters the warehouse and conceals himself in the shadows below the bridge. He does not see Holmes

Moriarty You seem remarkably concerned for this man Holmes.

Bella, shocked by her own outburst, does not answer

Why, my child? Why should you be so concerned at the fate of our life-long enemy?

Bella still pauses

Mrs Moriarty silently re-enters and sees Holmes on the upper level. She holds a revolver

Bella Mama once told me how she felt when she first met you. It was like seeing the tops of the Alps, she said ... cold, remote and beautiful ... unattainable, yet irresistible ... So far away, and yet so close.
Mrs Moriarty (*screaming*) Curse of my family, die! *Die!*
Bella (*looking up and shouting*) Mama, *no!*

A shot rings out and Holmes falls. Watson looks up in alarm

Watson Holmes!

There is no answer from Holmes. Watson wrests the gun from Mrs Moriarty's grasp. She runs to Moriarty, elated

Mrs Moriarty (*triumphantly*) James, my love, see! I have destroyed your mortal enemy, Sherlock Holmes!
Moriarty (*rising to his feet*) I think not, madam. (*He removes his disguise, revealing himself to be Sherlock Holmes*)

Everyone gasps, stunned

Watson Holmes! Well, I'll be damned!
Holmes (*calling out*) Are you all right, Wiggins?

The second "Holmes" — a slightly wounded Wiggins — props himself up on one arm and grins

Wiggins Just about, sir. (*To Mrs Moriarty*) You're lucky, lady! It only nicked me arm. Looks like the Lord abides in Wappin', an' all, Miss Bella!

Bella (*staring at Holmes in mingled disbelief and admiration*) That was a most cruel and callous trick, Mr Holmes!

Holmes I know of no pleasant way to outwit an entire family of Moriartys!

Bella (*scathingly*) I should have used a more lethal poison in the hot toddy.

Holmes But that would have denied me the inestimable pleasure (*his voice segués into the unmistakable tones of the Costermonger*) of our little knees up dahn the *Apples 'n' Pears*, wouldn't it, miss?

Bella loses her composure, and half-laughs in admiration of his audacity and ingenuity. Then she pulls herself together

Bella (*regaining her composure*) My father is dead, isn't he?

Holmes Yes, he is. Something I regret more than you will ever know. I have missed the old fellow confoundedly these past months. (*He takes out a pipe and stuffs it with tobacco*) But in you, Miss Moriarty, he has produced a dare-I-say "foelady" worthy of my steel ... Just tell me, I assumed you used the Wertenheimer Telescopic Ladder — to escape through the skylight.

Bella Of course.

Holmes (*delighted*) Good, good, good! I remember all the facts I ever learned about your father. There was a story about an Italian opera singer in Wakefield. Did your mother give you much assistance?

Bella (*modestly*) A little. The plan was mine.

Holmes I *knew* it. Brilliant! Congratulations! It has the stamp of genius ... you know, on the whole, Bella, I find your crimes far superior in artistic merit to your paintings.

Bella We thought we had planned the perfect murder.

Holmes (*putting the pipe back in his mouth, taking out a box of matches*) You reckoned without the perfect detective.

Bella We relied on the police to get you hanged!

Holmes That was hardly a fair gamble ... With Lestrade in charge, a miscarriage of justice was almost inevitable! I probably *would* have been hanged! If you'd wanted it done properly, you should have consulted *me*! (*He smiles in self-deprecation at his excess enthusiasm*)

Lestrade and his police reinforcements emerge quietly from their hiding place behind the crates

Lestrade chokes back his anger at Holmes's remark

Bella doesn't seem to see them. She moves towards Holmes

Bella I have been thinking ...
Holmes Pray go on.
Bella Seriously thinking. If your powers were ever to be married to the mind of a Moriarty — just imagine what a great leap forward there might be in the process of evolution!

Holmes looks at her, admiring, wondering, absorbing what she has just said. The music of "The Best of You, the Best of Me" builds romantically as they dare to contemplate the possibilities of her potent remark

The magical mood is predictably broken by the mundane droning voice of Lestrade, which now echoes pompously through the premises

Lestrade Do not move! Stay where you are, in the name of the law! I'll take that revolver, doctor.

Watson hands him the revolver. Mrs Moriarty suddenly lunges at Lestrade, grabs the gun and rushes up on to the bridge

Mrs Moriarty Bella, come!

Bella slowly follows her up on to the bridge

(*She holds the revolver pointed at Holmes's head*) This time there will be no mistake!

Bella has a split-second in which to comprehend, decide and act

Bella (*crying out*) Mama, *no!* (*She pushes out her arm to stop her mother*)

They struggle together. Mrs Moriarty is moving with such momentum that she loses her balance and both she and Bella plunge over the side of the bridge in an eerily similar replay of Moriarty's own death

As they disappear from view, the gun goes off. There is a huge explosion and a series of blinding flashes as the explosives go up

Watson and Lestrade hurry to where the bodies have fallen. They re-emerge slowly from the smoke-filled area

Watson (*sadly, to Holmes*) I'm afraid Mrs Moriarty finally has her wish to be reunited with the Professor ...

Holmes (*apprehensively*) And Bella? Is she ...?

Watson (*gravely*) It's too early to tell how she is, Holmes ... (*he looks up and smiles*) because she's not there! She's done it *again*! She's *gone*! What *can* you say about that girl?!

Holmes (*greatly relieved*) What indeed, Watson! She is remarkable! And I fancy we haven't seen the last of her!

Holmes and Watson exit

Lestrade (*still pompous, even in tatters*) She does have a way with her — I'll say that! But we'll be more than a match for her the next time, I promise you. You should have left all this to me, Holmes. Might have been a very different story ... Holmes? (*He looks around and sees that Holmes is gone*) Hmm ... He clearly doesn't want to deal with the humiliation of being outwitted by an adversary — (*smugly*) I could teach him a thing or two about that ... Come along men — don't hang about.

He exits grandly, followed by Tomkins and Bottomley

The Lights cross-fade to:

SCENE 9

Holmes's study

Holmes looks into space, reviewing recent events

We hear Bella as a voice-over

Song 22: A Million Years Ago — or Was It Yesterday? (Reprise)

Bella   (*off*) A million dreams ago —
                         Or was it one or two?

I dreamed a dream
And it was you —
Just a dream,
But it came true!
Don't come any closer —
Unless you can stay!

Unless you can stay!
Unless there's a way!
Unless you can say
It's forever —
And never
Go away!

Holmes (*reflectively*) What was it she said? *My* powers married to the
mind of a Moriarty! What a fascinating hypothesis!

Song 23: The Best of You, the Best of Me

The best of you —
The best of me —
To me would be the best
That there could ever be!

Unlikely pair
Though we may be,
We strike a special spark
For all the world to see.

Such dangerous games
We love to play —
And who will get the best of whom,
It's hard to say ...

*The music continues under as a Light comes up on Bella as she appears
on an upper level, carrying a small posy of bright red-purple flowers.
She looks sadly down at 221B Baker Street*

Bella   We lend the world
                   A little style —
                   And best of all,
                   We do it with a little smile.

Both   The best of times
                   Are ours together —
                   Though cynics say
                   The best is past,
                   We are the living proof
                   That someone knew
                   To save the best for last.

Bella   Like china tea,
                   The best of blends —
                   The kind that makes
                   The best of foes
                   The best of friends.

                   And to this brew,
                   If you agree,
                   We simply add
                   The rest of you —
                   The rest of me —

Both   The best of you —
                   The best of me —
                   Making thus
                   This wondrous plus —
                   The best of us!

Watson enters Holmes's study, looking gloomy

Holmes settles in the chair behind the desk, and the Light fades on Bella on the upper level

Bella exits

Watson (*dejectedly*) So she's gone! Dunno about you, but Moriarty or no, I shall miss her, damnit!

Holmes (*matter-of-factly*) Your sentimentality is commendable, Watson, but you would have paid for it with your life!

Watson (*looking seriously at Holmes*) Holmes ...

Holmes Yes, Watson?

Watson When she said that to you about evolution. You remember ...?

Holmes I do recall something ...

Watson You could never have possibly for a second considered ... *marriage* with a *Moriarty*?

Holmes (*considering*) Oh, I don't know. *Two* brilliant minds! ... (*He fantasizes for a moment, then smiles up at Watson*) No, I'm far better off with *yours*, old fellow.

Watson (*visibly moved*) Thank you, Holmes.

Holmes Please. Think nothing of it. Sit down, Watson. Why don't you take your old chair by the fireplace?

Watson sits. The sound of a piano-tuner hitting odd notes seeps into the room. Holmes abstractedly reaches out for his instrument-case

Watson (*sternly*) Holmes!

Holmes drops the instrument-case into the waste-paper basket. He smiles and pulls out a pipe instead

Holmes Very well, doctor. Henceforth it shall be tobacco.

Watson I got Mrs Hudson to put a pound of shag in the slipper.

Holmes How very thoughtful of you! You know, Watson, I fear London may become a dull sort of place again without the sparkling company of our newfound and dangerous friend, Miss Bella Moriarty.

Offstage the piano-tuner starts to play a plaintive, off-key reprise of "The Best of You", underscoring Holmes's bleak mood

   D'you hear that, Watson?

Watson It's the piano-tuner. Just arrived as I came in.

Holmes I know. But listen!

Watson (*humming a few notes*) Da-da-da-dum ... Da-da-da-dum ... pretty!

Holmes And hopelessly out of tune! (*He stands up. Excitedly*) Have you ever heard of such a thing? A tone-deaf piano-tuner? (*He hurries over to the door and opens it*)

As he opens the door, the outer street-door of 221B slams shut

Mrs Hudson approaches and hands Holmes the same small posy of bright red-purple flowers that Bella was carrying

Mrs Hudson The piano-tuner left you these flowers, sir. Isn't that nice?

Holmes takes one look at the flowers and smiles broadly. The music starts to bubble under his growing excitement

Holmes Of course! *Belladonna velenosa*! Perfect!
Watson (*blinking*) Beg your pardon, Holmes?
Holmes *Belladonna velenosa* has two meanings, Watson. In Italian it means "poisonous beautiful lady". We know it better as deadly nightshade, the most poisonous of all beautiful flowers. It contains the poison atropine ... C-seventeen H-twenty-two W-three N ... and so, I suspect, does Miss Bella!
Watson What does it all mean, Holmes?
Holmes It means deep waters, Watson!
Watson (*musing*) "Deep Waters" ... Nice title! (*He writes it down*)

Music begins under the following

Holmes Wonderfully deep and mysterious waters! One thing is for sure, my friend. Our old enemy's not dead! ... Or should I say our *new* enemy? (*He goes to the window and looks out with a challenging smile*) Are you there, Moriarty? Is the game still on? Then sir, or madam, I am ready for you! Sherlock Holmes is ready!

Song 24: I Shall Find Her (Reprise)

I have no way of predicting
When or where we're meant to meet!
When I'll challenge this enchantress —
This Delilah of deceit!

But there's one thing that is certain —
That the moment will be sweet!

Watson   Without a Moriarty,
Holmes is incomplete!

Holmes   And when I find her, this I know —
I shall never, never, ever let her go!

Full Company (*off*) And when I find her, this I know —
I shall never, never, ever let her go!

Black-out

The Lights come up to full as the Irregulars and the Full Company pour on from every direction

Song 25: Sherlock Holmes (Finale)

Curtain call reprise

Company   Sherlock Holmes
Is certainly the greatest man there is!
The great achievements of the day
Are almost always *his*!
And I believe, in years to come,
When memories grow dim,
A lot of things he *hasn't* done
Will be ascribed to him!
The greatest deeds will be ascribed to him!
Without him, England's future would be grim!

Sherlock Holmes
Must surely be the genius of his day!
When people finish speaking of him,
They haven't a thing to say!
And one day he will take his place
In history's favourite tomes —
The one and only Sherlock Holmes!

The egotistical, slightly mystical,
Incorruptible, indestructible,

One and only Sherlock Holmes!
Sherlock Holmes!
All said and done —
Sherlock Holmes!
There's only one —
Sherlock Holmes!

The CURTAIN *slowly falls*

NB The curtain call can also contain a further full company reprise of one
complete chorus of "Down the Apples 'n' Pears"

FURNITURE AND PROPERTY LIST

ACT I
PROLOGUE

Off stage: Newspapers (**Irregulars**)
2 suitcases, one marked S. H. containing deerstalker and ulster, one
    with a bullet-hole (**Watson**)
2-wheeled trolley (**Holmes** as **Porter**)

Personal: **Moriarty:** silver-knobbed cane/sword-stick
Watson: black arm-band, half-hunter watch (worn throughout)
Moran: handcuffs

Set during set change on p. 2: pile of luggage

ACT I
SCENE 1

On stage: 2 armchairs
Fireplace
Table with chemical equipment
Pipe racks
Books
Coal scuttle with tobacco slipper and cigars
Pistols
Bust of Socrates with a pipe
Sword-stick
Leather violin case containing a syringe
Bell rope
Sabre

Off stage: Top hat (**Jarndyce**)
Gloves (**Jarndyce**)
Walking stick (**Jarndyce**)
Letter containing playing card (**Mrs Hudson**)

ACT I
SCENE 2

On stage: Fishmonger's stall
            Large salmon
            Sack containing golden mace

Off stage: Handcuffs (**Policemen**)

ACT I
SCENE 3

Re-set: as for Act I, Scene 1

Set: List on mantelpiece
            Pen

Off stage: Card on a salver (**Mrs Hudson**)

Personal: **Lestrade:** Notebook, pen

ACT I
SCENE 4

On stage: Banner
            Potted ferns
            Gallery seat
            Empty frame

Off stage: Catalogue (**Watson**)

Personal: **Watson:** cheroot, lighter

ACT I
SCENE 5

Nil

ACT I
SCENE 6

Reset: as for Act I, Scene 1, only more tidy

Set: Kettle on hob
Tray with whisky decanter, sugar, lemon, glasses
Flowers
Holmes's dressing-gown

Off-stage: Feather duster (**Mrs Hudson**)
More flowers (**Bella**)
Tray of watches (**Holmes** as **Blind Man**)
White cane (**Holmes** as **Blind Man**)

Personal: **Holmes** (as **Blind Man**): black-lensed spectacles

ACT I
SCENE 7

Off stage: Polishing cloth (**Mrs Hudson**)
Reed instrument (**Mrs Moriarty**)
Box of chocolates (**Watson**)

Personal: **Bella: Holmes's** deerstalker, ulster and pipe

ACT I
SCENE 8

Personal: **Bella:** locket

ACT I
SCENE 9

On stage: 2 easels with canvases
Fireplace
Stove with kettle, whisky bottle, glass, etc.
Holmes's deerstalker and ulster
Throne-like chair
Paints
Brushes
Matches
Incense
Key in door lock
Sketches of Moriarty (hanging behind a curtain)
Portrait of Moriarty

Off stage: Sword-stick (**Holmes**)
              Bella's locket (**Holmes**)
              Ladder (**Mrs Moriarty**)
              Bullseye lanterns (**Policemen**)

ACT II
SCENE 1

Re-set: as for Act I, Scene 9

Set: Chalk line

Personal: **Holmes:** handcuffs, pipe, corked phial
              Lestrade: notebook, pen, handcuffs, key, scarf

ACT II
SCENE 2

Off stage: Newspapers (**Wiggins, Irregulars**)

ACT II
SCENE 3

Re-set: as for Act I, Scene 1

Personal: **Holmes** (as **Chelsea Pensioner**): walking stick, corked phial with
              hot toddy, spotted handkerchief
              Watson: notepad, pen

ACT II
SCENE 4

Nil

ACT II
SCENE 5

On stage: Slab tables
              Shrouded cadavers
              Bottle of port and 2 port glasses (in drawer)

Off stage: Clipboard and pen (**Assistant**)
               Umbrella (**Watson**)

ACT II
SCENE 6

Nil

ACT II
SCENE 7

Off stage: Coffee trolley with cups, coffee pot, etc. (**Bella**)
               Instruments (**Salvation Army**)
               "Wanted" notice and pins (**Bottomley** and **Tomkins**)
               Fruit barrow (**Holmes** as **Costermonger**)

Personal: **Bella:** pince-nez glasses, coin
               Wiggins: large gold pocket-watch
               Holmes: envelope (in pocket)

ACT II
SCENE 8

On stage: Racks with shotguns and pistols
               Explosives cases

Off stage: Wheelchair (**Holmes** as **Moriarty**)
               Rug (**Holmes** as **Moriarty**)

Personal: **Mrs Moriarty:** money, revolver
               Holmes (as **Moriarty**): dark glasses, pipe, tobacco, matches

ACT II
SCENE 9

Re-set: as for Act I, Scene 1

Personal: **Bella:** posy of red-purple flowers

LIGHTING PLOT

Interior and exterior settings
Practical fittings required: gas lamps for Act I, Scene 9

ACT I, PROLOGUE
To open: Exterior lighting for the Reichenbach Falls

Cue 1	**Watson:** "HOLMES!"	(Page 2)
	Fade; when ready, bring up to Victoria Station effect	

Cue 2	**Mrs Hudson** slams the door	(Page 8)
	Black-out	

ACT I, SCENE 1
To open: Slowly fade up on Holmes's rooms

No cues

ACT I, SCENE 2

Cue 3	**Irregulars:** "Anything you want to know!" 3rd time	(Page 21)
	Cross-fade to Holmes's room	

ACT I, SCENE 3

Cue 4	**Holmes** snaps the blade back into the sword-stick	(Page 29)
	Cross-fade to Royal Academy	

ACT I, SCENE 4

Cue 5	**Irregulars:** "But who's complaining?"	(Page 35)
	Cross-fade to the streets of London	

ACT I, SCENE 5

No cues

ACT I, SCENE 6
To open: Change to Holmes's rooms

Cue 6   **Holmes** and **Bella** storm out of the room   (Page 47)
             Cross-fade to outside of 221B Baker Street

ACT I, SCENE 7

Cue 7   **Irregulars:** "I shall find her ..."   (Page 53)
             Cross-fade to the streets of London

ACT I, SCENE 8

Cue 8   **Holmes** exits after **Bella**   (Page 56)
             Fade to black-out

ACT I, SCENE 9
To open: Fade up to artist's studio effect. Night

Cue 9   **Bella** turns down the gas lamps   (Page 59)
             Dim lighting

Cue 10   **Policemen** turn up the gas lamps   (Page 63)
             Increase lighting

ACT II, SCENE 1
To open: Bring up artist's studio effect. Night

No cues

ACT II, SCENE 2
To open: Change to exterior lighting

Cue 11   **All:** "... can they catch Sherlock 'Olmes?!"   (Page 70)
             Cross-fade to Holmes's rooms

ACT II, SCENE 3

Cue 12   **Mrs Hudson:** "Truly — lousy — life!"   (Page 78)
             Cross-fade to somewhere in London

ACT II, SCENE 4

No cues

ACT II, Scene 5
To open: Bring up interior lighting

Cue 13   **Watson** exits   (Page 85)
              *Cross-fade to the River Thames embankment; street
                 lamp effect*

ACT II, Scene 6

Cue 14   **Mrs Moriarty** and **Bella** exit   (Page 88)
              Cross-fade to the Apples 'n' Pears *pub*

ACT II, Scene 7

Cue 15   **Holmes** and **Watson** exit   (Page 101)
              Cross-fade to deserted warehouse

ACT II, Scene 8

Cue 16   A huge explosion   (Page 107)
              A series of blinding flashes

Cue 17   **Lestrade** exits with **Tomkins** and **Bottomley**   (Page 108)
              Cross-fade to **Holmes's** *rooms*

ACT II, Scene 9

Cue 18   **Holmes:** "It's hard to say ..."   (Page 109)
              Spot on **Bella**

Cue 19   **Watson** enters   (Page 110)
              Fade spot on **Bella**

Cue 20   **Full Company:** "... ever let her go!"   (Page 113)
              Black-out; after a pause bring up to full

EFFECTS PLOT

ACT I

Cue 1   To open   (Page 1)
              Sound of wind, roar of raging water, swirling mists

Cue 2   The lights come up on Victoria Station   (Page 2)
              Sound of steam trains, whistles, slamming of carriage doors

Cue 3   **Holmes** swings a suitcase into the air   (Page 3)
              Rifle shot, followed by a police whistle and running footsteps

Cue 4   To open Scene 1   (Page 8)
              Melancholy violin music

Cue 5   **Holmes** stops playing   (Page 8)
              Cut violin music

Cue 6   **Holmes** returns to the violin   (Page 8)
              Violin music

Cue 7   **Holmes** stops playing   (Page 9)
              Cut violin music

Cue 8   **Holmes** returns to the violin   (Page 10)
              Violin music

Cue 9   **Holmes** stops playing   (Page 10)
              Cut violin music

Cue 10   **Watson:** "Replace."   (Page 39)
              Doorbell

Cue 11   To open Act I, Scene 8   (Page 53)
              Swirling mists (throughout scene)

Cue 12   **Bella:** "... against the light."   (Page 58)
              An operatic female voice sings from "Vendetta"

ACT II